Supply Chain Risk Manage
in the Apparel Industry

Apparel is one of the oldest and largest export industries in the world. It is also one of the most global industries because most nations produce for the international textile and apparel market. The changing global landscape drives cost volatility, regulatory risk and change in consumer preference. In today's retail landscape, media and advocacy groups have focused attention on social and environmental issues, as well as new regulatory requirements and stricter legislations. Understanding and managing any risk within the supply chain, particularly ethical and responsible sourcing, has become increasingly critical.

This book first gives a systematic introduction to the evolution of SCRM through literature review and discusses the importance of SCRM in the apparel industry. Second, it describes the life cycle of the apparel supply chain and defines the different roles of the value chain in the apparel industry. Third, it identifies the risk factors in the Apparel Life Cycle and analyzes the risk sources and consequences and finally, extends the importance of selection of the suppliers and develops a supplier selection model and SCRM strategies solution by data analysis and case studies.

Peter Cheng is the co-founder and Chairman of Hanbo group. He obtained his Executive Master of Business Administration (EMBA) degree in 2014 and Doctorate of Business Administration (DBA) degree in 2018 at the City University of Hong Kong. His research interests are supply chain risk management and management science. He has been an important figure in the co-founding of both the Hong Kong Apparel Society Limited (HKAS) and Hanbo Enterprises Limited, and his experience in offshore production bases includes Sri Lanka, Cambodia, Kenya, Honduras, Jordan, Bangladesh, Vietnam, Myanmar and Indonesia. He also conceptualized the SMART supply chain management model.

Yelin Fu is Post-Doctoral Fellow at College of Economics, Shenzhen University. He has two PhDs from the College of Business, City University of Hong Kong, and the School of Management, University of Science and Technology of China. He has published papers in *Annals of Operations Research, International Journal of Logistics Management, International Transactions in Operational Research, Journal of Engineer Manufacture* and *International Journal of Systems Science*.

Kin Keung Lai is the Changjiang Chair Professor of the International Business School of the Shaanxi Normal University, China. He was previously Chair Professor of Management Science at the City University of Hong Kong. His main areas of research interests are operations and supply chain management, financial and business risk analysis and modelling using computational intelligence. He is Founding Chairman of the Hong Kong Operational Research Society of Hong Kong and is also currently President of the Asia Association on Risk and Crises Management.

Routledge Advances in Risk Management
Edited by Kin Keung Lai and Shouyang Wang

For more information about this series, please visit www.routledge.com/Routledge-Advances-in-Risk-Management/book-series/RM001

Supply Chain Risk Management in the Apparel Industry

Peter Cheng, Yelin Fu and Kin Keung Lai

Routledge
Taylor & Francis Group

LONDON AND NEW YORK

First published 2018
by Routledge
2 Park Square, Milton Park, Abingdon, Oxon OX14 4RN

and by Routledge
605 Third Avenue, New York, NY 10017

First issued in paperback 2020

Routledge is an imprint of the Taylor & Francis Group, an informa business

British Library Cataloguing-in-Publication Data
A catalogue record for this book is available from the British Library

Library of Congress Cataloging-in-Publication Data
Names: Cheng, Peter (Peter Lap-yin), author. | Fu, Yelin, author. |
    Lai, Kin Keung, author.
Title: Supply chain risk management in the apparel industry / by
    Peter Cheng, Yelin Fu and Kin Keung Lai.
Description: Abingdon, Oxon ; New York, NY : Routledge, 2018. |
    Series: Routledge advances in risk management ; 12 | Includes
    bibliographical references and index.
Identifiers: LCCN 2018003020 | ISBN 9781138787865 (hardback) |
    ISBN 9781315314174 (ebook)
Subjects: LCSH: Clothing trade—Risk management. | Business
    logistics. | International trade.
Classification: LCC HD9940.A2 C44 2018 | DDC
    687.068/7—dc23
LC record available at https://lccn.loc.gov/2018003020

ISBN 13: 978-0-367-50411-3 (pbk)
ISBN 13: 978-1-138-78786-5 (hbk)

Typeset in Galliard
by Apex CoVantage, LLC

Contents

Figures

Tables

Preface

Apparel supply chain management service providers play an increasingly important role in the apparel industry in assisting apparel brand owners and retailers lower the production costs and improve the efficiency of the apparel supply chain. Apparel brand owners and retailers have found it increasingly difficult to differentiate their products from their competitors' products due to rapid technology development in the apparel industry, which made it easier to imitate and copy designs. As a result, they have tried to win market share through minimizing the production costs and shortening the production lead times. In addition, since the WTO's Agreement on Textiles and Clothing took effect on 1 January 2005 and quota restrictions on the textiles and clothing trade amongst members were removed, there has been a movement of apparel manufacturers being concentrated to certain regions, including the Greater China region, Bangladesh, Vietnam, Cambodia and Myanmar. This has led to a growth in the number of apparel supply chain management service providers in these countries, which are looking to provide access to those manufacturers more efficiently and in a more cost-effective manner.

Apparel supply chain management service providers in the Greater China region can provide a wide range of products and services along the apparel supply chain, including apparel product design and development, fashion trend collation and sampling, sourcing of raw materials, production order and management, quality control, inventory management and logistics management. The product scopes offered include woven wear and knitwear products.

Based upon a case study in a Hong Kong apparel supply chain service provider – Hanbo Enterprise Holdings Limited – various risks along the apparel supply chain should attract more attention, which can be broadly categorized into: (1) risks relating to operation business; (2) risks relating to apparel industry; (3) risks relating to conducting business in the PRC; (4) risks relating to conducting business in countries other than the PRC. This book makes the first effort to take risk management into account in apparel supply chain management and develops a family of methods to deal with both supply and demand uncertainty.

Chapter 1 starts by providing a detailed introduction about the current status of the apparel industry in Hong Kong, the concept of the apparel supply chain and the theory of supply chain risk management.

Chapter 2 offers the readers a precise picture of the concept, application and theory of supply chain risk management, which summarizes various effective methods in the extant literature.

Chapter 3 conducts an empirical study to obtain experts' preferences on vendor evaluation and selection criteria, and it proposes a sophisticated mathematical model to derive the exact weights associated with each criterion on the basis of survey.

Chapter 4 proposes several objective methods to determine weights with respect to each criterion: variation of coefficient, Shannon entropy, distance-based method and group decision making.

Chapter 5 considers the fact that different decision makers may have different preference among the evaluation criteria and develops an inter-valued decision matrix to implement vendor selection using the SMAA-2 method.

Chapter 6 gives a robust optimization method to support supplier selection in the presence of uncertain demand.

Chapter 7 presents the other robust optimization scheme to help make production capacity planning decisions when the material utilization is uncertain.

Chapter 8 conducts a case study in Hanbo Enterprises Holdings Limited for the purpose of verifying the significance of supply chain risk management in apparel industry.

Peter Cheng
Hanbo Enterprises Holdings Limited, Hong Kong
City University of Hong Kong, Hong Kong

Yelin Fu
Shenzhen University, China

Kin Keung Lai
Shaanxi Normal University, China

1 Introduction

1.1 The apparel industry in Hong Kong

As a major manufacturing and import–export sector in Hong Kong, the apparel industry is composed of 657 manufacturing companies hiring 4,763 workers and 14,630 import–export establishments providing 79,950 positions as of March 2017. Hong Kong's geographic boundary has never constrained the development of the forward-looking apparel industry. The majority of clothing manufacturers have established offshore production facilities in an attempt to cut down on operation costs. Relocation of production facilities offshore has, however, given rise to a largely steady decline in the number of apparel manufacturers in Hong Kong. Hong Kong is not only a leading production center but also a hub for apparel sourcing globally. Companies doing garment trade in Hong Kong are experienced in fabrics procurement, sales and marketing, quality control, logistic arrangements, clothing designs and international and national rules and regulations. The professionalism that they command and the combined services offered are not easily matched elsewhere. They altogether form one of the largest groups involved in import–export trade in Hong Kong.

Starting on 1 January 2009, textile and clothing products originating in China no longer require any import license or surveillance document before entering the EU. Meanwhile, textile and clothing shipments to the US made on or after 1 January 2009 are no longer subject to any quotas. Under the Mainland and Hong Kong Closer Economic Partnership Arrangement (CEPA), the mainland has given all products of Hong Kong origin, including clothing items, tariff-free treatment starting on 1 January 2006. According to the stipulated procedures, products which have no existing CEPA rules of origin will enjoy tariff-free treatment upon applications by local manufacturers and upon the CEPA rule of origins being agreed and met. The promulgated rules of origin for clothing items to benefit from CEPA's tariff preference are basically similar to the existing rules governing Hong Kong's exports of these products. Generally speaking, the principal manufacturing process of cut-and-sewn garment is sewing of parts into garments. If linking and/or stitching is/are required, such process/processes must also be done in Hong Kong.

For a piece-knitted garment, if it is manufactured from yarn, the principal process is knitting yarn into a knit-to-shape panel. If the piece-knitted garment is manufactured from knit-to-shape-panels, the principal process is linking of knit-to-shape panels into a garment. If stitching is required, it must also be done in Hong Kong. Hong Kong clothing companies are reputable for Original Design Manufacturer (ODM) and Original Equipment Manufacturer (OEM) production. They are able to deliver apparel articles with high quality standards in short lead time, as foreign importers and retailers request clothing suppliers to tighten up supply chain management to ensure the ordered merchandise reaching the store floor at the right time. Increasingly, Hong Kong clothing companies, the established ones in particular, have shown enthusiasm for brand promotion.

In recent years, traditional apparel markets, such as the US, the EU and Japan, have rendered clothing exporters from developing countries, including ASEAN and Bangladesh, more preferential market access, which has in turn impaired the competitiveness of Hong Kong and mainland manufacturers. Along with rising labour costs and stricter environmental regulations on the Chinese mainland, an increasing number of Hong Kong and mainland clothing manufacturers have relocated their production of lower-end and mass products to Southeast Asian countries like Bangladesh, Vietnam, Cambodia and Indonesia. Their manufacturing operations on the mainland are now focussed on more sophisticated and higher value-added items or urgent orders.

Hong Kong's total exports of clothing shrink by 10 percent year-on-year in the first five months of 2017 after a 15 percent decrease in 2016. From January to May 2017, Hong Kong's domestic exports of clothing slid by 46 percent, while re-exports fell by 10 percent.

Among the major export destinations, Hong Kong's clothing exports to the US decreased by 9 percent in the first five months of 2017, while those to the EU were down by 12 percent. Clothing exports to major EU markets including the UK, Germany, France and Italy fell by 13–33 percent. However, clothing exports to the Netherlands rose by 7 percent. Taken together, sales to the US and the EU accounted for more than 60 percent of Hong Kong's total clothing exports. Meanwhile, sales to Japan dropped by 8 percent, whereas the Chinese mainland market showed a 6 percent decrease in January–May 2017.

As for products, Hong Kong's exports of woven wear fell by 9 percent year-on-year in the first five months of 2017. Exports of knitted wear decreased by 10 percent, whereas clothing accessories and other apparel articles declined by 9 percent and 10 percent, respectively.

Hong Kong's clothing manufacturers have comprehensive knowledge about sourcing and products. They are able to understand and cater to the preferences of the dispersed customer bases. Exporters also have good knowledge of international and national rules and regulations governing clothing exports, such as rules of origin, tariff rates and documentation requirements. Cut, make and trim (CMT) arrangements are common, although many Hong Kong manufacturers have moved to higher value-added activities such as design and brand development, quality control, logistics and material sourcing.

A few well-established local manufacturers have entered into the retailing business, either locally or in overseas markets. Many of them have retail networks with their own labels in major cities around the world including Beijing, London, New York, San Francisco, Shanghai, Singapore, Sydney, Taipei and Tokyo. Some well-known manufacturing retailers include Baleno, Bossini, Crocodile, Episode, Esprit, G-2000, Giordano, I.T, JEANSWEST and Moiselle.

As a global sourcing hub in Asia, Hong Kong attracts a number of international trading houses and major retailers. Buyers sourcing from Hong Kong include American and European department stores (e.g. Macy's, JCPenney, Federated, Karstadt Quelle, C&A), discount stores (e.g. Sears, Target and Carrefour), specialty chains (e.g. The Gap and The Limited), mail order houses (e.g. Otto and Great Universal Stores) and e-tailers (Zalora and YOOX). Many international premium designer labels – such as Calvin Klein, Donna Karen, Ralph Lauren, Tommy Hilfiger and Yves Saint Laurent – source clothes in Hong Kong through their buying offices or other intermediaries.

Hong Kong's fashion designers have been gaining worldwide reputation for their professional expertise, sensitivity to current trends and ability to blend commercialism with innovation. In February 2017, four Hong Kong designers, Cynthia Mak, Xiao, Harrison Wong and Polly Ho, were invited to showcase their Fall/Winter 2017 collections at the Show of Fashion Hong Kong during New York Fashion Week. Furthermore, medium to high-priced fashion clothing bearing Hong Kong designer labels is being sold/has been sold in renowned department stores and e-tailing platforms such as Bloomingdale's, Ferd.com, Net-A-Porter and Macy's.

In the 2016–17 Budget announced on 24 February 2016, the then-Financial Secretary John Tsang unveiled that HK$500 million has been earmarked to further the development of the fashion industry through (1) strengthening the promotion of local fashion designers and emerging fashion brands in Hong Kong and overseas; (2) establishing an incubation programme for fashion designers, drawing on the experience of other fashion capitals like London, New York and Seoul; and (2) setting up a resource center to provide technical training and support for young designers.

Trade fairs and exhibitions remain common places for buyers and suppliers of clothing to congregate. To establish connections and explore market opportunities, Hong Kong manufacturers and traders have involved themselves actively in international shows led by the Hong Kong Trade Development Council (HKTDC), including the ones in Beijing, Budapest, Chengdu, Dalian, Dubai, Dusseldorf, Hong Kong, Moscow, Mumbai, Paris, Tokyo, Warsaw, Istanbul and Jakarta. 'Hong Kong Fashion Week' is organized twice a year and attracts international suppliers and buyers to participate in the exhibition. Organized by HKTDC, 'World Boutique, Hong Kong' was the first independent event in

Hong Kong dedicated to promoting designers' collection and brands from around the world. To better align the event with the international fashion trade calendar, the fair, from 2016 onwards, was rescheduled from January to September and re-named CENTRESTAGE, serving as a dedicated marketing platform for international and regional brands, ready-to-wear and designer labels to showcase their collections.

Online shopping is increasingly popular in Hong Kong's major clothing markets, including the Chinese mainland where there are 467 million online shoppers in 2016. Across the board, clothing is among the most purchased items online. Last year, online clothing sales were estimated to have accounted for 41 percent of the total online shopping turnover on China's largest online shopping day that fell on 11 November (also called the Single's Day). Also, a recent PwC survey indicates that Chinese consumers are the most inclined to online clothing shopping, with more than 72 percent of the Chinese respondents saying that they prefer buying clothes through the internet.

The growing variety of online shopping sites such as Taobao (www.taobao.com) in China and ASOS Marketplace in the UK (www.marketplace.asos.com), in conjunction with the bloom of group shopping and mobile retailing, is expected to boost online shopping and sales further. The continuous improvement of third-party payment such as Alipay by Alibaba Group and WeChat Pay by Tencent also helps popularize online shopping. It is estimated that global retail e-commerce sales will more than double from the current level and exceed US$4 trillion by 2020. This trend has also encouraged the development of some online shopping technologies such as virtual fitting, video shopping and mobile snapshot for clothing.

Private or house labels, in essence, have become an increasingly effective marketing tool among garment retailers, especially when many consumers in developed markets still remain conservative in view of the nascent economic recovery. In order to differentiate as well as upgrade the image of their products, major retailers have started to put a stronger emphasis on their own labels. Renowned retailers such as H&M, Marks & Spencer, Orsay, Palmers, Pimkie, Springfield and Kookai have owned their private labels. As consumers desire to have private labels on everyday garments like jeans, accessories and T-shirts, the doors are also open to the supply of these clothing items to private label owners.

Consumers are becoming more practical, thoughtful and socially conscious. The drive to embed sustainability within the clothing industry will likely bring forth new materials and innovative ways of production, while the concept of a circular economy will become more widely applied throughout the supply chain by committing to such ideas as end-of-life collection and closed-loop fashion products to enable the reuse and recycling of textile fibers and fabrics. Against this backdrop, clothing manufacturers have increasingly become certified to traceability standards such as OE Blended, OE 100 standard and the Global Organic Textile Standard (GOTS). Meanwhile, the number of GOTS certified facilities demonstrated a substantial increase from 3,814 in 2015 to 4,642 facilities across 63 countries last year. Reputable clothing stores like Nike, Adidas, H&M, C&A, Walmart and Anvil Knitwear have responded by expanding their assortment of sustainable clothing.

The rapid expansion of mainland's economy has drawn the attention of both Hong Kong and foreign clothing companies. While some well-established foreign players including C&A, Uniqlo and H&M are seeking to expand in the lower-tier cities, those which are not yet present on the mainland are working hard to mark their inroads. For instance, Victoria's Secret is about to open a flagship store in Causeway Bay, leveraging Hong Kong as a springboard to go across the border. Going hand-in-hand with the market expansion, Chinese consumers are becoming more fashionable and brand-conscious.

Consumers in mature markets continue to resume spending on fashion products but still opt for items that offer comfort, function and value-for-money – and nothing too radical. Longevity remains an important element, while items with recognizable brands and decent quality are still highly sought-after.

One of the major driving forces of the clothing market appears to be the children in the coming years, particularly in the developed markets. The global market for children's wear is forecast to reach US$186 billion by 2020. In light of the economic recovery, parents are becoming more willing and able to pamper their children with more exquisite apparel.

Men are increasingly concerned about the clothes which come to their wardrobes. According to Euromonitor, the men's clothing market is forecast to exceed US$490 million by 2020, up from US$ 411 million in 2016. Moreover, men have been spending more on their outfits each year for more than a decade now, thanks partly to the growing popularity of online menswear shopping that showed an annual sales growth of more than 17 percent between 2010 and 2015.

An ageing population has become a common phenomenon in many developed countries in Europe, Japan and in the US. The United Nations projects that populations aged 60 or over in more developed regions accounts for 22–33 percent of their respective population. Elderly people constitute a major market segment called the 'silver market'. Supported by savings, social security benefits and pensions, many elderly people have rather strong spending power. A survey conducted by the Japanese government also shows that people who are 60 years old and above possess almost three times the financial assets of those in the 40–50 age group.

The plus-size market has been an area of growth for many years, and the trend is expected to continue, particularly in the US and UK. For instance, it is estimated that the average American woman is about 25 pounds heavier than she was in 1960, whereas the population of obese Americans is forecast to reach 42 percent by 2030. To tap the trend, some renowned brands such as Liz Claiborne, Ralph Lauren, Tommy Hilfiger and H&M have already responded by offering merchandise in larger sizes.

Clothes made of stain-resistant and wrinkle-free fabrics are well received in the market. It is estimated that over a quarter of apparel is now made of easy-care fabrics, and its popularity is expected to continue. While major apparel brands like Dockers and Liz Claiborne have already marketed extensively easy-care clothes, major hypermarkets, like Walmart, also offer more merchandise of such quality.

Thanks to the growing awareness on health and quality of life, the demand for functional clothing is climbing. Along with the rapid development of functional clothing innovation, apparel with various functions can easily be found in the market. Anti-UV, anti-ray, good sweat management, thermal insulation and self-cleaning are examples of how material technology is being applied to the garment industry.

The growth of technology allows consumers to search the internet and find a way to create their own custom-made outfits. This is the modern way to express their creativity by making their own fashion designs and clothes. In response, some reputable clothing stores like Nike, Adidas and Walmart have started to sell personalized apparel, while companies with smaller business allow consumers to customize clothes and accessories with their own design online.

Concerns over both dressing green and product comfortability are always on the rise, making clothes made of natural fibers popular among consumers, especially in the developed markets. According to the latest Cotton Incorporated Lifestyle Monitor Survey, 73 percent of US consumers believed that better quality garments are made from all natural fibers and 65 percent of them were willing to pay more for it.

Besides, more and more fashion brands adopt green techniques/designs to increase efficiency and reduce waste in the production process. For instance, H&M has initiated 'H&M Conscious', promising more efficient use of natural resources and adoption of 3Rs principle in production, while fashion brand G-Star RAW has invented and used in its collections Bionic Yarn, an eco-friendly fabric made of fibers derived from recycled plastic bottles found in the ocean.

1.2 Apparel supply chain

1.2.1 *Factors affecting demand and production of apparel products*

1 *The economic situation.* During times of an economic upturn, consumers both in the global market and in the US will generally have a higher average annual disposable income and are more willing to spend more on pursuing a higher standard of living in terms of, for example, following fashion trends. This increases the demand for apparel products both in the global market and in the US market which will increase the demand for apparel supply chain management service providers. In times of economic downturn, such as during the financial downturn in 2008 and 2009, the average annual disposable income of consumers is generally lower and consumers are more inclined to spend only on daily necessities, leading to a decrease in demand for apparel products and a drop in the sales revenue of the apparel industry in the global market and the US market.

2 *Changes in the age structure of the population and consumer preferences.* As seen in the Greater China region, an aging population could lead to an increase in demand for looser-fitting styles of apparel, as consumers generally have expanding waistlines as they age whilst a stable/increasing birthrate, as seen in the US during 2010 and 2011, generally leads to growing demand for apparel products for babies.

3 *Availability of raw materials in the Greater China region and Southeast Asia.* A shortage of a particular raw material could lead to an increase in its price and subsequently increase production costs. Apparel manufacturers may have to consider substitute raw materials if the cost increase is prohibitive. Apparel supply chain management service providers usually charge the retailer based on the estimated manufacturing costs of apparel products, so a change in the manufacturing costs due to the availability of raw materials may lead to a change in contract prices.

4 *Demand for apparel products in the global market, the US and the EU.* Any increase or decrease in demand for apparel products in these markets could affect the apparel manufacturing industry in the Greater China region and Southeast Asia. The US and the EU are major export destinations of apparel products worldwide, contributing an estimated 21.5 percent (US$327 billion) and 24.9 percent (US$379 billion) of the total expenditure of apparel imports worldwide, respectively.

5 *Increase in labour costs.* An increase in labour costs could lead to rising production costs, which affects the apparel manufacturing industry in the Greater China region and Southeast Asia. Manufacturers may relocate their factories to other countries with lower labour costs, weakening the competitiveness of the country they leave. The average monthly salary per person in the apparel manufacturing industry in the Greater China region has increased approximately 15.0 percent since 2011 to HK$1,300 in 2012. In comparison, the average monthly salary in 2012 for countries in Southeast Asia, such as Bangladesh (HK$300), Cambodia (HK$600) and Vietnam (HK$800), is lower.

6 *Support from the government and implementation of trade policies and agreements in major apparel exporting countries.* This has helped to boost apparel manufacturing. Support from the government could be from tax relief, suspending tariffs or export duties, assuring financing and liquidity for enterprises. The Trans-Pacific Partnership (**TPP**) is a trade agreement currently being negotiated by 12 countries, including the US and Vietnam. Under TPP, Vietnam's exports would have the tax rate of 0 percent instead of the current rate of 17.3 percent. As the US is one of the members of TPP, many apparel companies or manufacturers who mainly export products to the US have established their factories in the southeastern Asian countries which are also members of TPP, including Vietnam. The Regional Comprehensive Economic Partnership (**RCEP**) is an initiative aimed at linking the ten members of the Association of Southeast Asian Nations (**ASEAN**), which counts Cambodia, Vietnam, Myanmar and Indonesia amongst its members, and the group's free trade agreement partners include the Greater China region.

1.2.2   Overview of the apparel supply chain management service in the Greater China region

Apparel supply chain management service providers play an increasingly important role in the apparel industry in assisting apparel brand owners and retailers lower the production costs and improve the efficiency of the apparel supply chain. Apparel brand owners and retailers have found it increasingly difficult to differentiate their products from their competitors due to rapid technology development in the apparel industry, which made it easier to imitate and copy designs. As a result, they have tried to win market share through minimizing the production costs and shortening the production lead times. In addition, since the WTO's Agreement on Textiles and Clothing took effect on 1 January 2005 and quota restrictions on the textiles and clothing trade amongst members were removed, there has been a movement of apparel manufacturers being concentrated to certain regions including the Greater China region, Bangladesh, Vietnam, Cambodia and Myanmar. This has led to a growth in the number of apparel supply chain management service providers in these countries, which are looking to provide access to those manufacturers more efficiently and in a more cost-effective manner.

Apparel supply chain management service providers in the Greater China region can provide a wide range of products and services along the apparel supply chain including apparel product design and development, fashion trend collation and sampling, sourcing of raw materials, production order and management, quality control, inventory management and logistics management. The product scopes offered include woven wear and knitwear products.

1.2.3   Number of apparel supply chain management service providers in the Greater China region

The total number of apparel supply chain management service providers in the Greater China region is expected to reach an estimated 516 in 2013 from an estimated 280 in 2008, at a CAGR of about 13.0 percent. Despite a growth in the number of apparel supply chain management service providers during the previous few years, the number of apparel supply chain management service providers in the market is still limited. In 2013, the total number of apparel supply chain management service providers in the Greater China region is less than 5 percent. of the total number of apparel manufacturers in the Greater China region. A strong capability in apparel supply chain coordination and well-established relationships with the apparel manufacturers are important criteria to becoming an apparel supply chain management service provider in the Greater China region. As competition increases in the apparel retail market, apparel brand owners and retailers tend to focus on their core business and outsource apparel supply chain management services to apparel supply chain management service providers. It is expected that there is great potential for the apparel supply chain management service providers to grow.

1.2.4 Revenue of apparel supply chain management service providers in the Greater China region

The total revenue of the apparel supply chain management service industry in the Greater China region has grown rapidly from approximately HK$170.6 billion in 2008 to approximately HK$323.6 billion in 2013, at a CAGR of 13.7 percent. Although rising labour costs in the Greater China region, coupled with the appreciation of the RMB, has seen a massive relocation of production of lower-end manufacturing away from the Greater China region, and to countries in Southeast Asia, the Greater China region remains the production base of choice for more sophisticated and higher value-added apparel products and orders which require a very quick turnaround time. It is expected that the total revenue of the apparel supply chain management service industry in the Greater China region will grow at a slightly faster rate at a CAGR of around 14.4 percent from approximately HK$369.6 billion in 2014 to approximately HK$553.0 billion in 2017.

1.2.5 Production value of the apparel industry in the Greater China region and selected regions of Southeast Asia

From 2008–2013, the total production value of the apparel industry in the Greater China Region, Bangladesh, Cambodia, Vietnam and Indonesia grew at a CAGR of 12.4 percent, 12.8 percent, 11.9 percent, 16.0 percent and 9.6 percent respectively. From 2014–2017, the total production value of the apparel industry in the Greater China Region, Bangladesh, Cambodia, Vietnam and Indonesia is expected to grow at a CAGR of 12.9 percent, 13.6 percent, 17.4 percent, 17.6 percent and 13.9 percent respectively.

1.2.6 Average price of apparel supply chain management services and apparel production per contract in the Greater China region

It is expected that the average price of apparel supply chain management services per contract will drop slightly due to a reduction in order quantity per contract from 2014 to 2017. The average price of apparel supply chain management services per contract grew significantly from an estimated HK$551,700 in 2008 to an estimated HK$987,600 in 2013, at a CAGR of about 12.4 percent, whilst the average price of apparel production service per contract increased from an estimated HK$477,400 to an estimated HK$613,500 at a CAGR of 5.1 percent over the same period. The average price of apparel supply chain management services per contract depends heavily on the average price of apparel product service per contract; however, the apparel supply chain management services industry has shown greater flexibility reflected by the greater volatility of the average price of apparel supply chain management services per contract.

It is expected that the average price of apparel supply chain management services per contract will drop annually by about 2.0 percent from 2014 to 2017, whilst the average price of apparel production services per contract will see a mild annual growth of about 1.5 percent over the same period. This will likely be due to increasingly fierce competition in the global apparel industry, leading apparel brands and retailers to reduce the quantity of their orders per contract in order to gain more flexibility in meeting fast changing consumer preferences.

1.2.7   Historical price trends of raw materials and final products

The global average annual price of cotton increased from approximately HK$71.4 per ton in 2008 to approximately HK$90.3 per ton in 2013. The average price of cotton in the global market reached an all-time low towards late 2008 and early 2009, due to decreasing demand from the apparel industry, as the average household disposable income decreased following the global financial crisis in 2008. The average price of cotton in the global market reached an all-time high in 2011 due to occurrences of flooding in major cotton-producing areas, including regions in the PRC, Australia and Pakistan. As the supply of cotton decreased as a result of such occurrences of flooding, the price of cotton increased.

From 2008 to 2013, the average price of cotton in the Greater China region was at its lowest in 2008 and 2009, reflecting the decreased demand for apparel products during the economic downturn. However, 2010 and 2011 saw a sudden surge in the price of cotton, where according to the China Cotton Association, the domestic demand for cotton was over 10 million tons in 2010. Surging demand for cotton coupled with shrinking local production pushed the average price of cotton upwards, peaking at about HK$28,723.9 per ton in 2011. The increase in price triggered an increase in the average price of apparel supply chain management services per contract to approximately HK$1,591,500 in 2011, an increase of around 67.4 percent compared to 2010. Parts of the increase in costs were shifted to manufacturers or retailers. Apparel supply chain management service providers may charge their customers based on the estimated manufacturing costs by purchase orders. Therefore, an increase in the price of key materials (e.g. cotton) will increase the price charged by apparel supply chain management service providers to their customers. Meanwhile, the average price of fabric in the Greater China region decreased from approximately HK$60.0 per kg in 2008 to approximately HK$50.6 per kg in 2013, decreasing at a CAGR of approximately 3.3 percent. The decrease in the average price of fabric in the Greater China region was mainly caused by the decline in the demand for woven wear and increasing demand for cut-and-sewn knitwear.

1.2.8 Factors affecting the apparel manufacturing industry in Southeast Asia

Bangladesh

Bangladesh has a competitive advantage by being able to offer high production capacity, with approximately 3.6 million workers and 5,000 apparel factories. However, without modern equipment and machinery, the country's manufacturing efficiency is restricted and this means that manufacturers are unwilling to place orders for more sophisticated products with manufacturers here. Another problem that Bangladesh faces is the poor infrastructure, in terms of transport and utilities, which can hinder the development of their apparel manufacturing industry and increase the logistical costs of an apparel supply chain management service provider.

Cambodia

Cambodia is export-dependent and during the economic downturn of 2008 and 2009, Cambodia's apparel manufacturing industry was affected as global demand for apparels dropped significantly. As a result of this, approximately 63,000 jobs were lost as around 50 factories were closed. Cambodia is hampered by a lack of a skilled workforce, and this has hindered Cambodia from moving into high-end manufacturing. While the current minimum wage was increased from about HK$585 to HK$775 per month on 31 December 2013, unions and workers have demanded an increase in wages to HK$1,241 per month. The strikes have led to a decrease in the productivity of workers and are likely to affect exports of apparel products in the short-term and long-term.

Myanmar

As labour costs rise in neighboring countries, more customers are starting to source their apparel goods from Myanmar. Gaining sufficient orders will be essential for the development of Myanmar's apparel manufacturing sector. Due to the country's limited interactions with the international market, the transfer of expertise and technology from foreign countries has been limited. The exchange of skills and knowledge from other countries is vital for improving the overall manufacturing efficiency and productivity. An unstable power supply means that manufacturing factories in Myanmar often lose electricity and have had to depend on diesel generators, which generally cost four times more than regular electricity, leading to extra costs being added to their initial expenses.

Indonesia

Although Indonesia has a slightly higher minimum wage than neighboring countries, it remains a popular choice for international customers because of the broad variety of fabrics on offer in Indonesia. However, the technology and equipment in Indonesia is outdated, which leads to lower labour productivity and Indonesia faces increasing competition from the Greater China region since the PRC joined ASEAN in 2010.

Vietnam

Manufacturers in Vietnam face comparatively lower capital requirements for producing apparel compared with producing machinery and electronics. Although Vietnam's apparel manufacturing industry has grown rapidly in the past few years, benefiting from foreign investors such as South Korea and Taiwan, the country's heavy reliance on imported raw materials such as cotton and yarn has created an imbalance in terms of investment and production, making the apparel manufacturing industry unsustainable. With a shortage of skilled labour, apparel manufacturing in Vietnam has been restricted to basic design styles focussing on woven wear and children's clothing in particular, restricting sourcing opportunities for apparel supply chain management service providers.

1.2.9   Competitive landscape and competitive advantage

The apparel supply chain management service provider industry in the Greater China region is highly fragmented, with more than 482 and 516 service providers in 2012 and 2013 respectively. The top ten apparel supply chain management service providers accounted for about HK$139.9 billion, representing approximately 49.3 percent of the total market revenue of the apparel supply chain management service industry in 2012.

Competitive advantages

According to the Industry Expert Report, there are mainly five key advantages of our company's brand compared to our competitors, including (1) a well-established reputation and long-term relationship with our customers – this allows us to have a more stable income and strong brand reputation in relation to which we have received awards from our customers and this increases the possibility of gaining orders from customers; (2) our experienced management team – the knowledge and experience of our management team enables us to respond quickly to the fast-changing trends in the apparel industry; (3) our extensive supply network – this covers the Greater China region and Southeast Asian countries, including Bangladesh and Cambodia, which enables us to respond quickly to industry demands and maintain a stable supply of apparel products for our customers, which in turn gives our customers confidence in our strengths and abilities; (4) our full range service offering – this means that our customers can rely on us for all their apparel supply chain management service needs; and (5) two of our top ten customers are top US retailers or brands. Together, they accounted for about HK$315.4 billion of retail sales in 2012 in the global market. Having such retailers or brands as part of our customer base allows us to have a more stable income. Our competitive advantages are not quantifiable.

Factors of competition

1   *Long-term relationships with apparel brand owners or retailers and manufacturers.* Apparel brand owners or retailers tend to cooperate with apparel supply chain management service providers that they are familiar with in order to ensure that their quality standards are met. A well-established relationship can ensure a more stable supply of apparel products and reduce lead times through familiarity with how each other works, e.g. when orders are placed, capacity bookings.
2   *Full service capabilities.* Apparel supply chain management service providers who can offer a full range of services are likely to stand out from their competitors, as apparel brand owners and retailers are increasingly looking for full service capabilities. Full-service capabilities could include product design and development, fashion trend monitoring, sample production, raw materials sourcing, managing and allocation production to third-party manufacturers, quality control, logistics management etc.
3   *Certifications and standards.* International and regional certifications can be representative of the quality of services and products offered by apparel supply chain management service providers. Apparel manufacturers are more likely to cooperate with apparel supply chain management service providers who can provide qualified services and products.

*Barriers of entry for apparel supply chain service providers
in the Greater China region*

1   *Increasing dependence on long-term relationships.* Since the removal of the quota system for textiles and apparel products in January 2005, there has been an increasing reliance on building long-term relationships between apparel supply chain management service providers and manufacturers. Under the quota system, many trades were carried out under short-term relationships whereas, apparel supply chain management service providers now restructure their network of suppliers with the aim of building long-term strategic partnerships with their key suppliers.
2   *Full supply chain capability.* With the growing retailer demand for fast changing fashion, apparel supply chain management service providers are required to demonstrate full service capabilities which new entrants may struggle to adapt to, or may not have the resources to offer. Significant time and resources are required to build a reputable status in such a competitive and fast moving industry.
3   *Reliability.* New entrants may struggle to build their customer base as apparel brand owners and retailers tend to return to apparel supply chain management service providers which they have engaged previously and which they see as reliable. Without the opportunity to build their own reputations of reliability, new entrants may struggle to capture new customers, or maintain any which they already have.

*Opportunities for apparel supply chain management service
providers in the Greater China region*

1   It is anticipated that there will be more and more apparel retailers looking
     to source raw materials from new suppliers globally. Unfamiliarity with
     certain geographical locations could lead to more market opportunities for
     supply chain management service providers who already have an established
     network with local suppliers and manufacturers.
2   The 12th Five-Year plan of the PRC is an opportunity to enhance the
     competitiveness of PRC's apparel industry supply chain, through a focus
     on improving the quality standard system, credit system and evaluation of
     the market's efficiency.
3   There is an increasing acceptance by US consumers for apparel that is
     manufactured in Southeast Asia. Whilst the Greater China region retained
     its leading position in the US's top five apparel import countries in
     terms of actual volume, Vietnam, Bangladesh and Indonesia account for
     number 2 to number 4 respectively. The position of the Southeast Asian
     countries is largely attributed to the ability to offer manufacturing at
     lower costs, primarily due to lower wages compared with the Greater
     China region.

*Threats for apparel supply chain management service providers
in the Greater China region*

1   The apparel supply chain management service industry in the PRC has been
     established for a number of years and the overall processes and personnel
     are becoming more mature. It is harder for apparel supply chain manage-
     ment service providers to differentiate themselves from their competitors
     unless they have already developed a positive reputation for delivering
     effective services.
2   Despite the increasing acceptance of apparel manufactured in Southeast
     Asia, there is an increasing trend for US domestic designers and retailers
     to move part of their production back to the US. This is mostly due to
     the rapid increase in labour wages, safety issues and scheduling problems
     in Asian factories. Further, 75.0 percent of local American consumers have
     shown willingness to pay for apparel which is made in the US, presenting
     another incentive for US domestic designers and retailers to reshore pro-
     duction to the US.
3   With the improving conditions in safety and labour relations in apparel
     manufacturing factories in Mexico, there is an expectation for an increase
     in demand for import of apparel products from Mexico to the US.
4   Currency fluctuations could affect demand for apparel supply chain manage-
     ment services. An appreciation of the currency in countries where our
     company engages third-party manufacturers increases labour costs and cost
     of raw materials. A depreciation in the currency in countries where our

customers are based reduces the demand for apparel products, as the price of the apparel products increases. As a result, currency fluctuations may mean that there would likely be less demand from retailers to engage apparel supply chain management service providers.

5 Apparel supply chain management service providers who do not comply with the various security and custom inspections in the countries of origin, transshipment or destination of the apparel products may be subject to duties, fines or seizure of apparel products.

As one of the largest and oldest import and export industries, the apparel industry has been behaving as a crucial player in advancing the world economy, and it is typically recognized as an effective weapon to fight poverty and sources of social stress. Economically speaking, the apparel industry is an attractive segment for investment, trade and employment in both developing and developed countries. For instance, the US Department of Labor reported that the apparel manufacturing industry has provided the US with about 142,860 work positions in 2014, while the apparel industry of Sri Lanka employed around 15 percent of the total workforce and accounts for around 50 percent of the country's export.

Apparel trade has been exponentially growing since the 1970s, even though its development is practically restricted by some trade regulations. For example, Multi-Fiber Arrangement (MFA) made efforts to stipulate quotas for regulating apparel export to Canada, the US and some European countries starting in 1974, which was reflected by the World Trade Organization (WTO) with the Clothing and Textiles agreement between 1995 and 2005. Furthermore, two important incidents have significantly affected the landscape of global apparel sourcing. The first event is the quota system phase-out, which resulted in a large number of opportunities and challenges for both least-developed and developing countries, while the second incident is economic crisis brought by the bankruptcy of Lehman Brothers in September 2008, which motivated the importers in global trade to play new roles and construct new relationships in collaboration with their global business partners (Gereffi and Frederick, 2010). The characteristics of the apparel supply chain have been enumerated by Routroy and Shankar (2014) as follows: global supply chains, short product life cycle, demand volatility, long production period and distribution lead time, fierce competition, high product variety, large amount of SKUs, large degree of market segmentation, environmental concerns, shortage of supply flexibility and prediction errors. Meanwhile, the corresponding risk factors in apparel supply chain are summarized in Table 1.1.

The strategy of global sourcing has been used considerably in the last 30 years, which is recognized as a component of competitive advantage (Manuj and Mentzer, 2008; Jain et al., 2014). The advantages of global sourcing typically are comprised of a cheap workforce, inexpensive raw materials, more financing opportunity at a lower cost, a broader product market and extra inducements to attract foreign capital. Starting in the 1990s, China Mainland,

Table 1.1 Risk elements corresponding to the characteristics of apparel supply chains

Characteristics of apparel supply chain	Risk factors
Global supply chains	Outsourcing risks; supplier dependency; production lead time; distribution lead time; fluctuations in exchange rate; customs duty; supply chain complexity; government regulations
Demand volatility	Inability of supply; volatile demand; changes in customer tastes; sudden fluctuations; deterioration of service performance; loss of control; poor strategic development; loss of market share; market turbulence
Short product life cycle	Supplier dependency; information risks; higher product costs; forecasting errors
Long production and distribution lead time	Inability of supply; dependence risks; deterioration of service performance; loss of control
High competition	Competition changes
Large product variety	Inability of supply; supplier fulfillment errors; supplier dependency; order fulfillment errors
Large number of SKUs in a season	Risk of product obsolescence; sudden fluctuations
Environmental concerns	Government regulations; loss of customer confidence
High degree of market fragmentation	Volatile demand; changes in customer tastes; sudden fluctuation; loss of control
Inflexibility of supply source	Failure of the partnership; inability of supply; inflexibility of supply source; loss of competitive advantage with the supplier
Forecasting errors	Overestimating or underestimating; lack of sharing of crucial data

Source: Routroy and Shankar (2014).

Hong Kong SAR, South Korea and Taiwan were ready to outsource production arrangements through sub-contracting the clothing assembly to a number of Asian countries in which the wages were lower and export quotas were enough, for example, Sri Lanka, Vietnam and Bangladesh (Gereffi, 1999; Audet, 2004). Observed from the WTO global trade statistics on commodity (2010), the value of global apparel export was US$483 billion in 2014, an increase of 74 percent since the closing of the WTO Agreement on Textiles and Clothing in 2005. In recent years, Asian countries have gradually become the main exporters of apparel products. China, Vietnam, Bangladesh, Indonesia, Cambodia and India account for more than 50 percent of global apparel exports in 2014. During 2005 and 2014, apparel export has been exponentially growing with an increase in Vietnam (318 percent), Bangladesh (257 percent) and Cambodia (166 percent), whereas Hong Kong apparel export has decreased by 25 percent (Tables 1.2 and 1.3).

Table 1.2 Changes of global apparel export (in billon US dollars)

Reporter	1990	2000	2005	2010	2014	2014	% of total clothing export in 2014	Change % 2014/2005
World	108.13	197.93	278.26	353.41	459.66	483.28	100.00%	73.68%
China	9.67	36.07	74.16	129.82	177.41	186.61	38.61%	151.63%
European Union (28)	–	56.71	86.27	100.7	118.64	126.59	26.19%	50.21%
Bangladesh	0.64	5.07	6.89	14.85	23.5	24.58	5.09%	256.75%
Hong Kong, China	15.41	24.21	27.29	24.05	21.92	20.51	4.24%	-24.84%
Vietnam	–	1.82	4.68	10.39	17.15	19.54	4.04%	317.52%
India	2.53	5.97	8.74	11.23	15.54	17.74	3.67%	102.97%
Indonesia	1.65	4.73	4.96	6.82	7.69	7.67	1.59%	54.64%
United States	2.56	8.63	5.01	4.69	5.86	6.11	1.26%	21.96%
Cambodia	–	0.97	2.21	3.04	5.03	5.87	1.21%	165.61%

Source: http://stat.wto.org/Home/WSDBHome.aspx?Language=E

Table 1.3 Changes of global apparel import (in billon US dollars)

Reporter	1990	2000	2005	2010	2013	2014	% of total clothing import in 2014	Change % 2014/2005
World	112.24	203.10	279.41	369.42	481.11	540.03	100%	93.28%
European Union (28)	–	83.46	132.16	167.50	183.19	198.26	36.71%	50.02%
United States	26.98	67.12	80.07	81.94	91.03	93.16	17.25%	16.35%
Japan	8.77	19.71	22.54	26.87	33.63	31.16	5.77%	38.24%
Hong Kong, China	6.91	16.01	18.44	16.64	16.45	16.17	2.99%	–12.31%
Canada	2.39	3.69	5.98	8.31	9.95	10.08	1.87%	68.56%
Russian Federation	–	0.20	0.93	7.54	9.01	8.51	1.58%	815.05%
Korea	0.15	1.31	2.91	4.44	7.64	8.48	1.57%	191.40%
Australia	0.71	1.86	3.12	4.83	6.26	6.52	1.21%	108.97%
Switzerland	3.44	3.18	4.45	5.29	5.90	6.13	1.14%	37.75%
China	0.05	1.19	1.63	2.52	5.34	6.12	1.13%	275.46%

Source: http://stat.wto.org/Home/WSDBHome.aspx?Language=E

Globalization has unexpectedly resulted in a number of new challenges about production disruption and disperse suppliers along with the global apparel supply chain. Social media and advocacy groups have been paying increasing attention to investigate social, environmental and economic factors that would result in additional possibility of reputational risk. Meanwhile, the adoption of new regulatory items and the appearance of stricter legislations make the apparel supply chain face new challenges as well. Recent accidents and incidents reflected various risks within the apparel supply chain and urgently required effective risk management schemes as the first priority in global apparel sourcing.

In Bangladesh, a horrific fire accident in a garment factory killed 112 workers in November 2012, and in April 2013 1,100 workers lost their lives because of the collapse of the Rana Plaza building. Furthermore, garment manufacturers in Cambodia have been subject to the most frequent strikes in 2013, and there were over 131 strikes (GMAC[1]) for the purpose of requiring higher salaries and better social welfare. The loss caused by production disruption was estimated at about US$275 million. Those protests definitely resulted in some uncertain and unpredictable events in the apparel and shoe industries and then gave risk to purchase order (PO) reductions of about 20–30 percent in 2014. Moreover, hundreds of workers in Vietnam joined the anti-China activity at May 2014, and several irrational workers even seek to destroy factories by setting fires, which eventually brought about product supply disruption and investors' uncertainty to further invest in Vietnam.

In January 2015, SACOM (Students and Scholars Against Corporate Misbehavior) illustrated that the working conditions did not meet the required standards at the factories which produced apparel for UNIQLO. These events reflected the serious results from risks associated with both safety and labour standard compliance in the apparel industry, which then resulted in supply risk for buyers, demand risk for manufacturers from buyer/consumers, social and political risk and finally, it gave rise to economic risk. The aforementioned risks surely have severe negative impacts on workers, organizations' reputations and the whole supply chain efficiency. It is thereby significantly critical for global apparel supply managers to identify risk factors, evaluate the impact of risks and offer solutions to mitigate risks.

1.3 Supply chain risk management

Conventional vendor selection is usually performed based upon performance criteria, i.e., supply variety, quality, delivery time, etc. (Ho et al., 2010; Chai et al., 2013; Viswanadham and Samvedi, 2013). However, in an environment of global sourcing, a number of factors, including political, social and economic issues, as well as natural and manmade disasters, may inevitably result in disruptions. In other words, risk is receiving increased attention because more and more uncertain factors are influencing the whole supply chain. Due to the fact that risk management has become an important component of global sourcing, it is of great significance to identify all such risk factors and then provide solutions to implement risk management. The origination of risk could be diverse, and absolute risk mitigation is an infeasible solution. Furthermore, the vendor selection problem in the circumstance of globalization is essentially a Multiple Attribute Decision Making (MADM) or Multiple Criteria Decision Making (MCDM) problem, which should simultaneously consider many intangible and tangle performance factors in the evaluating and selecting process.

Some researchers have incorporated the concept of SCRM into vendor evaluation and selection. Wu and Olson (2008) summarize three scenarios of risk assessment alternatives in supply chain management: Data Envelopment Analysis (DEA), Multiple Objective Programming (MOP) and Chance Constrained Programming (CCP) models, and compare them with simulation analysis to facilitate supplier selection decisions. Wu and Olson (2010) develop a DEA Value-at-Risk (VaR) based model to perform risk analysis and management in the process of vendor selection. Supply risks in Enterprise Risk Management (ERM) are assessed. Ravindran et al. (2010) propose two choices of risk analysis models, namely, Value-at-Risk (VaR) and Miss-the-Target (MtT), to formulate Multiple Criteria supplier selection models considering supply risks, which are demonstrated using a real case study. Olson and Wu (2011) illustrate the usage of DEA, DEA-based simulation analysis and Monte Carlo simulation in terms of a risk-adjusted cost logic to implement vendor selection. Chen and Wu (2013) develop a Modified Failure Mode and Effects Analysis (MFMEA) approach to implementing supplier selection according to the viewpoint of SCRM, and they apply the Analytic Hierarchy Process (AHP) to calculate the weights associated with each criterion as well as sub-criterion for supplier selection. Viswanadham and Samvedi (2013) employ performance-based and risk-based criteria to formulate a Multiple Criteria supplier selection problem, which is solved by a two-stage analysis that involves the usage of fuzzy AHP and fuzzy TOPSIS.

As an apparel supply chain manager with over 30 years of working experience, I propose that the main purpose of this book is to share our solutions to the following questions with both partners and competitors in apparel industry:

1   What are the risk factors that influence the vendor selection in global apparel sourcing?
2   How will we measure the importance degree of risk together with other performance factors, such as finance, service, quality, cost, flexibility and partnership?
3   How will we implement vendor selection based upon these criteria?
4   How will the vendors be selected in the presence of uncertain demand?
5   How will the vendors determine the capacity in the presence of uncertain material utilization?

Note

1 Garment Manufacturers' Association in Cambodia.

2 Concept, application and theory of apparel supply chain risk management

2.1 Supply chain risk management

Although the terminology of supply chain risk management (SCRM) has been defined by many scholars and practitioners, I strongly agree with the following two viewpoints:

1 Supply chain risk management is "the implementation strategies to manage both everyday and exceptional risks along the supply chain based on continuous risk assessment with the objective of reducing vulnerability and ensuring continuity".

(Wieland and Wallenburg, 2012)

2 Supply chain risk management is "the management of supply chain risks through coordination or collaboration among the supply chain partners so as to ensure profitability and continuity".

(Tang, 2006)

On the strength of the above definitions with respect to SCRM, it is meaningful to review the existing SCRM literature in the following three dimensions:

1 identifying the factors of supply chain risk;
2 assessing the magnitude of supply chain risk; and
3 mitigating the outcomes of supply chain risk.

Jüttner et al. (2003) make an effort to identify a research agenda for the investigation of supply chain risk management and to present a reasonable definition. The extant studies about vulnerability examination and risk management along the supply chain have been reviewed. Finch (2004) reviews and conducts a secondary analysis of supply chain management literature, together with case studies to decide on whether large enterprises increase their exposure to risk with SMEs as partners in the supply chain. Tang (2006) provides a detailed literature review about different quantitative methods to manage supply chain risks and examines the existing supply chain risk management policies mentioned in previous publications along with real cases. Colicchia and Strozzi (2012) undertake a constructive literature network analysis of SCRM to study the procedure of knowledge creation, transformation and development according to a dynamics perspective. Heckmann et al. (2015) review the existing quantitative SCRM approaches, focussing on the definition, measure and modelling of supply chain risk. Ho et al. (2015) summarize and categorize SCRM research during 2003 and 2013; review the research status on supply chain risk definition, risk factors identification and risk mitigation schemes; and point out the potential research gaps. Rangel et al. (2015) conduct a literature survey on 16 risk classifications, including 56 risk types sorted by existing conceptual similarities. This literature review highlights the shortage of consensus about the risk types affecting a supply chain.

2.1.1 Supply chain risk identification

Neiger et al. (2009) develop a new value-focussed procedure engineering method to identify procedure-based supply chain risk management strategy for the purpose of increasing the both supply chain players as well as the whole supply chain. Tang and Musa (2011) present a publication review and conduct citation/co-citation analysis to examine the research development of SCRM between 1995 and 2009. This work guides the readers to identify and classify the risks associated with material, cash and information flows. Song et al. (2016) propose a rough weighted decision making and trial evaluation laboratory (DEMATEL) to identify risk elements under the framework of sustainable supply chain management. The advantages of the present model include flexibly manipulating the vagueness and ambiguity involved in risk analysis. Wu et al. (2017) propose the fuzzy and grey Delphi models to identify the attributes of risks, using big data techniques to transform them into a manageable scale.

2.1.2 Supply chain risk assessment

The techniques associated with assessing supply chain risk can be either quantitative or qualitative. Steele and Court (1996) develop a conceptual method to assessing supply risk, wherein the first stage is to estimate the probability of a risky event occurrence (low, medium and high chance), and the second is to estimate the likely problem duration based on previous experience. Michalski (2000) introduces a supply risk assessment process proposed by Microsoft and Arthur Anderson, namely, the comprehensive outsource risk evaluation (CORE) system. Zsidisin et al. (2004) discuss, provide analysis and obtain common topics about supply risk assessment methods from an agency theory perspective. Tummala and Schoenherr (2011) present an overall and coherent method based on Supply Chain Risk Management Process (SCRMP) to assessing and managing risks in supply chains. Vilko and Hallikas (2012) propose fundamental research concepts and results considering risk identification and mitigation with respect to multimodal supply chains. This is illustrated using Monte-Carlo-based simulation. Tazelaar and Snijders (2013) first replicate the 'process-performance paradox' exists in the circumstance of assessing operational supply risks, and demonstrate how this paradox would be recognized as the result of adjusting the interplay between assessment performance and expertise. In order to provide a landscape of proactively managing supply chain risks, Chand et al. (2015) perform a comparative study using MCDM approaches, ANP and a multiple objective optimization by ratio analysis (MOORA) technique. Nakandala et al. (2017) develop a hybrid model involving fuzzy logic (FL) and hierarchical holographic modelling (HHM) techniques, in which risk is identified by the HHM model and assessed using the qualitative risk assessment model and the fuzzy-based risk assessment method. A case study about a fresh food supply chain company is conducted to show the effectiveness of the developed model.

2.1.3 Supply chain risk mitigation

Christopher and Lee (2004) and Kleindorfer and Saad (2005) consecutively develop a conceptual framework combining risk evaluation and risk mitigation, and then perform an empirical study using the data during 1995 and 2000 on contingencies in the US Chemical Industry. Implications for management system design are discussed to manage supply chain disruption risk. Cucchiella and Gastaldi (2006) develop a real option method to increase the level of flexibility and reduce supply chain risk in terms of decreasing the damages deriving from uncertain sources. Blome and Schoenherr (2011) develop a multiple case-study analysis to give a number of propositions on how firms manage supply risks in economic and financial crisis, and they comment on how different risk management methods have shifted. Khan and Yurt (2011) employ the multiple case-study analysis involving 15 cases in seven industries to investigate how decision makers evaluate the risks about global sourcing and what reactions to be employed for mitigating those risks. Diabat et al. (2012) use interpretive structural modelling (ISM) to identify various risks in a food supply chain, which are categorized into five clusters and mitigated. Micheli et al. (2014) develop a quantitative decision support system for choosing the right supply chain risk mitigation schemes. The proposed analytical mechanism is on the basis of stochastic integer linear programming method, which includes supply chain managers' judgments using utility functions and fuzzy-extended pairwise comparisons. Pradhan and Routroy (2014) propose a complete and structured methodology to analyze supply chain risk and develop supply chain risk mitigation solutions and is demonstrated in a manufacturing environment. Aqlan and Lam (2015) propose a method based upon bow-tie analysis and optimization techniques to quantify and mitigate supply chain risks, which considers risk interconnections and identifies the best integrations of mitigation strategies with budget constraint. Ambulkar et al. (2016) examine personal knowledge management elements that influence the result of supply chain risk mitigation. Ge et al. (2016) construct an integrated optimization–simulation framework denoting the novel Canadian wheat supply chain, for the purpose of determining cost efficient varietal testing strategies. Ghadge et al. (2017) present a risk sharing contract to mitigate the risks arisen from price volatility and demand fluctuation in a globalized business context. A real automotive case study is conducted to provide insights on buyer–supplier relationships.

2.2   Vendor selection

Vendor selection is the procedure through which the purchasers identify, assess and collaborate with vendor (Beil, 2010). This topic has received substantial attention in both decision analysis and supply chain management research and is becoming a fruitful research problem for operations research and management science fields. Weber et al. (1991) review 74 papers related to vendor selection problem since 1966 and emphasize the used criteria and analytic methods. Ho et al. (2010) exhaustively review the individual and integrated decision-making approaches between 2000 and 2008 to aid the supplier selection problem. Chai et al. (2013) complementarily provide a comprehensive literature review about the decision-making tools assisting vendor selection between 2008 and 2012, which classifies the mentioned techniques into three groups: MCDM techniques, artificial intelligence (AI) techniques and mathematical programming techniques.

The contemporary supply chain management requires decision maker to maintain strategic partnership with few but trustworthy suppliers (Ho et al., 2010), which effectively reduces the materials purchasing costs and improves the competitive advantages (Ghodsypour and O'Brien, 2001). Therefore, besides conventional price factor, promising supplier selection policy should also rely on a broad spectrum of quantitative and qualitative criteria including quality, delivery, flexibility and lead time, and others (Chen et al., 2006). Dickson (1966) has considered 23 criteria during the process of the purchasing manager determining supplier selection.

In this subsection, we review some representative methods in the existing literature that address vendor selection problem. Weber and Current (1993) identify 23 criteria for the Multiple Criteria vendor selection problem, and they develop a multiple objective method to analyze the balance in the Multiple Criteria vendor selection problem. Mandal and Deshmukh (1994) use Interpretive Structural Modelling (ISM) to implement supplier selection. Kasilingam and Lee (1996) provide a mix-integer programming method to choose vendors and decide on the purchase order (PO) scales, considering the quality of provided parts, the stochastic demand, the transportation and purchasing related costs, the cost to establish candidates and the cost with respect to handling parts with poor quality. Weber et al. (1998) make efforts to show how information from multiple objective programming and DEA can be combined in certain conditions to generate tools for selecting and negotiating with vendors. Petroin and Braglia (2000) facilitate vendor selection on the basis of a multivariate statistical approach, namely, principal component analysis, which employs information derived from eigenvalues to integrate different ratio measures calculated by each input and each output. Tam and Tummala (2001) formulate an AHP-related method to select proper vendors in the telecommunications system, which is typically a complicated multi-person and multi-criteria decision problem. Talluri and Narasimhan (2003) propose a max–min method on the basis of productivity while considering vendor performance volatility measures, which generates a nonparametric statistical technique to effectively identify a group of selected vendors. Teng and Jaramillo (2005) develop a simple, flexible and easy to implement supplier evaluation and selection considering five sets to reveal the performance of an international supplier from the US textile and apparel supply chain. Kumar et al. (2006) apply a fuzzy goal programming method to look for solutions to the multi-objective supplier selection problem, where some of the coefficients are fuzzy in real life. Sucky (2007) develops a dynamic decision-aiding method to facilitate strategic supplier selection on the basis of the rationales of hierarchical planning. Ng (2008) propose an easy-to-understand and simple-to-implement method to implement the Multiple Criteria vendor selection. Lin et al. (2010) develop a new integrated MCDM method to handle the complicated and interactive supplier assessment and selection issue, which is demonstrated in a Taiwan semiconductor company. Azadnia et al. (2015) present a combined approach including a rule-motivated weighted fuzzy approach, fuzzy AHP and multiple objective programming to choose sustainable vendors and allocate orders in a multi-period, multi-product, lot-sizing problem. Fu, Lai, Miao, and Leung (2016) aggregate different decision makers' preferences over multiple criteria through a distance-based method, which effectively reduces the discrepancies among different decision makers.

2.3 Robust optimization

The term 'robust optimization' encompasses several streams of work to protecting the decision makers against stochastic uncertainty and parameter ambiguity (Gabrel et al., 2014). The fundamental idea behind the first stream of robust optimization is to consider the worst-case scenario without specific distribution assumptions. Soyster (1973) pioneered the work on robust optimization by requiring that all uncertain parameters reach their worst-case value, which was deemed to be overconservative in practical implementation. Ben-Tal and Nemirovski (1998, 1999, 2000) made some improvements by employing an ellipsoidal uncertainty set to adjust the level of conservatism, and they presented tractable mathematical reformulations. Bertsimas and Sim (2003, 2004) addressed uncertainty by defining a polyhedron for each parameter and then proposed a concept of 'budget-of-uncertainty' to control conservatism. Thiele (2004) provided a tractable framework for supply chains and revenue management problems subject to uncertainty requiring little information of the underlying probability distributions, and they investigated the structure of the optimal solutions. Düzgün and Thile (2010) pointed out that a single range for each parameter still leads to overly conservative results, and then they described uncertain parameters using multiple ranges. Denton et al. (2010) developed robust allocation of surge blocks to operating rooms considering uncertain duration of surgical procedures. The second stream of work followed a scenario-based framework, in which the uncertainty was modelled through the use of a number of scenarios and then stochastic programming formulations were presented (Mulvey et al., 1995). The presented robust optimization method has been widely applied in the areas of revenue management (Lai and Ng, 2005), logistics (Leung et al., 2002), production planning (Leung and Wu, 2004) and bottleneck generalized assignment problems (Fu, Sun, Lai, Leung 2015). The drawback of this approach is that accurate probability data are extremely hard to obtain in practice, particularly for distributions varying over time. The third stream is developed by Ben-Tal and Nemirovski (2000) and Lin et al. (2004), who formulated a deterministic robust counterpart, given the magnitude of uncertainty of data, infeasibility tolerance and reliability levels when a probabilistic measurement is applied. The appealing advantages of their approaches are linearity, applicability and tractability and ease in controlling the level of conservatism.

3 A subjective method for vendor selection

3.1 Introduction

The apparel industry is recognized to be the world's second largest industry. Global sourcing strategy has been widely used in apparel supply chains because of increasing differences in material and labour costs among countries, advanced communication technologies and area-specific skill specialization (Jain et al., 2014). The main reason for global sourcing is not only cost reduction, but also focussing on core competencies, while the primary purpose of global sourcing strategy is to discover not only the vendor's competitive edges, but also the comparative location advantages of different regions in worldwide competition (Ravindran et al., 2010). Therefore, the increasingly tight connections that various vendors prefer definitely requires a more sophisticated selection process. In other words, vendor selection, consisting of identification and assessment of the appropriate vendors, has turned into a crucial activity of global sourcing. During the cooperation with global vendors, purchasers should take into consideration both opportunities and threats, due to the fact that global sourcing inevitably reduces control capabilities and increases uncertainty. The first goal of the present thesis is to identify the specific risk elements in the apparel supply chain, which is begun with the following two real cases raised in the apparel industry.

3.1.1 Case 1: Bangladesh's apparel industry tragedies

As the world's second largest apparel exporter, Bangladesh produces most of the international brands of clothes. There exist about 5,000 factories and more than 4 million workers in the Bangladesh apparel industry. The annual exports are estimated at about US$20 billion , which accounts for nearly 80 percent of Bangladeshi total annual export. The specific character, that is, low production cost, makes Bangladesh one of the most appropriate sites to perform outsourcing tasks.

However, several tragic incidents that happened in Bangladesh's apparel industry inspire not only different stakeholders to reconsider the current sourcing schemes, but also the government to implement ready-made garments (RMG) departments to develop economy in a socially responsible and sustainable manner.

Table 3.1 Accidents in the Bangladesh apparel industry

2013	8 workers were dead and 10 wounded in a fire disaster in Dhaka.
2013	More than 1,100 people lost their lives in a factory building collapse.
2012	Over 112 workers were gone in a fire incident occurred in Tazreen Fashion Limited.
2006	21 people were dead and 50 injured in the multi-story building collapse in Dhaka Industrial Park.
2005	More than 64 persons were dead in the building collapse of Spectrum Garments at April 2005.

The serious workshop collapse that occurred in Bangladesh on 24 April 2013 has killed more than 1,100 workers. However, this is not uncommon in many developing countries. More than 1,800 Bangladesh workers have lost their lives in fire disasters and factory building collapses in Dhaka since 2005. Being known for its lowest wage for workmen on this planet, most terrible working environment and frequent operation irregularity, Bangladesh was recognized as the eighth worst country with respect to industrial working atmosphere in 2012.

For the purpose of meeting the increasing demand for cost effective clothing required by European and American brands, plenty of factories are built out of the standards. Retailers try to cut down cost at the expense of workers' safety and health. Manufacturers and global buyers are criticized because of dangerous and terrible working conditions and unfair wages for workmen. By means of analyzing the related cases, this study seeks to identify risks existing in the apparel supply chain and their impacts.

Demand-related reputational risk

One of the most representative reputational risks with respect to retailers is the damage to their brands caused by the Bangladesh tragedy. Nowadays, customers are becoming more sensitive to enterprises' social responsibility. Without loss of generality, consumers that are demanding for apparel products take into account CSR as well. Therefore, the manufacturing process and fashion brand are unexpectedly required to be socially responsible. In line with the findings of several of the world's largest and most successful apparel retailers risen in the 1990s, issues including the absence of labour rights and the employment of child labour may give rise to long-term damage to the market value brands, the sales quantity and a company's reputation.

The occurrence of reputational risk should be carefully taken into account when making any business decisions, particularly in the fields that a company is lacking direct management and control. In spite of the fact that financial motivation and operational convenience are the key drivers in business decision making, the significance of reputational risk factors should be endorsed.

Compliance risk

In real business management, the working environment and the workers' safety guarantee belongs to compliance issues. The Rana Plaza accident not only highlights the necessity of re-examining the current compliance and standards, but it also inspires various NGOs, third-party compliance programs and company-specific efforts to make rigorous standards and implementation schemes without any tolerance. For the purpose of addressing compliance risks, an assessment process should be implemented to evaluate all operation activities along the supply chain. Better understanding of operational regulations and standards, and increased supply chain transparency, would effectively help apparel retailers and the corresponding suppliers realize their compliance risk management objectives.

Supply risk

Various events including natural hazards, worker strikes and shortages of raw materials, may inevitably lead to supply disruption and delayed deliveries. As the primary apparel supplier on our planet, Bangladesh is the major sourcing center for the industry's largest markets, such as Europe and North America. Retailers and customers from these markets may be significantly affected by the occurrence of supply disruption. The bullwhip effect suggests that retailers and customers are more susceptible to supply disruptions. On the other hand, supply disruption may also affect the way that the consumers, the media and other stakeholders perceive CSR. Network relationships between suppliers and sub-contractors could create a unified safety culture to construct an ethical working atmosphere along the whole supply chain. For the ease of managing supply disruptions, retailers should identify appropriate criteria to implement vendor selection. Therefore, developing an appropriate and effective vendor selection model is necessary for apparel supply chain managers to effectively mitigate risks in the process of apparel sourcing.

3.1.2 Case 2: the strikes of Cambodia garment workers: political risk

The Cambodia apparel industry has experienced too many frequent strikes in 2013. Workers have organized over 131 strikes up to November to require higher salaries and more welfare. The whole garment industry has to be closed for two weeks between late December and early January 2014 because of illegal protests to require the rise of wages. Resulting from this production interruption, the loss of sales was estimated at about US$200 million , and the real damage to property destruction was reported at US$75 million. In addition, those protests may result in unpredictability and uncertainty in the apparel industry. Purchase orders posted by buyers would be reduced or even cancelled to get rid of these risks.

Table 3.2 Risk identification in apparel sourcing

Demand risk	Supply risk	Environmental risk
Demand volatility; Demand predication; Consumer preference change; Short life cycles; Innovative competitors.	Suppliers reliability; Consolidation in supply markets; Supply cost; Quality issues; Potential disruption; Lead-time & delivery.	Natural disasters; Terrorism and war; Strikes; Regulatory changes; Trade policy/rules changes; Political instability; Economic fluctuation; Reputational risk; Compliance risk.

Operational risk	Network risk
Manufacturing yield variability; Inflexible processes; Equipment reliability; Limited capacity; Outsourcing key processes.	Asymmetric power relationships; Poor visibility; Inappropriate rules that distort demand; Absence of planning and forecasting; Bullwhip effects; Information management risk.

Source: Tang, 2006; Manuj and Mentzer, 2008; Tang and Musa, 2011.

On the basis case study in apparel industry and literatures review, different forms of risks in apparel sourcing are listed in Table 3.2. Further research will be performed to identify the risks sources/drivers and how to mitigate these risks.

Substantial changes have been undertaken in the apparel industry during the last 20 years, especially with respect to global sourcing and intensified competition. The demand prediction in the apparel industry is not easy to implement because consumers sometimes make purchasing decisions according to their tastes, lifestyles, incomes and others. On the other hand, the retail market is also dramatically changing, caused by the fluctuant pricing of raw materials and increasing labour cost, diminishing economics and volatile market demand. All of these make supply chain risk management the top priority of apparel manufacturers and retailers. Nowadays, supply chain management is facing more and more risk because the supply network is sufficiently complicated, which is revealed as various forms of uncertainties arisen in both supply and demand sides (Christopher and Lee, 2004).

Because of the observation that the current supply chain is more complex in the global market, it is of great significant to handle emerging supply chain risks with a proactive approach, and thus to improve efficiency and effectiveness. Risks may be found in any stage and in any step along the supply chain and also make significant impacts. The risks are usually supply risk, process risk, demand risk, information risk and environmental risk.

3.2　The proposed method

We begin by enumerating the criteria for vendors in apparel supply chain based upon the literature review and consultation with industry experts from the Hong Kong Apparel Society Limited. The literature (see Weber and Current, 1993); Ho et al. (2010); Chai et al. (2013)) has identified the common criteria associated with vendor selection, namely finance, quality, delivery, flexibility and partnership. Even though there exist some different descriptions for these criteria, the exact meaning of them is identical. On the other hand, researchers and practitioners specified in apparel supply chain management are gradually paying attention to the risk criterion for vendor selection (Routroy and Shankar, 2014). This is motivated by the occurrence of supply disruption, demand disruption, natural hazards and others, in the whole apparel supply chain, which result in serious economic and reputation loss for the stakeholders in the apparel industry.

3.2.1　Finance

Finance is an important criterion in the process of vendor selection. Buyers tend to assess the vendor through comparison of the cost. The attributes that affect cost typically include freight cost, product price and custom duties. Financial stability is another important factor that affects buyers' decisions.

3.2.2　Quality

Quality is another important criterion for vendor selection. Product quality can be identified as defect rate, passing rate and return rate.

3.2.3　Delivery

With respect to the vendor selection problem, the manufacturer should be able to control the delivery schedule arrangement on the basis of the customer's request. As an important criterion for vendor selection, delivery usually should be connected with on-time delivery and satisfactory fill rate.

3.2.4　Flexibility

Vendor's flexibility to make appropriate changes according to a customer's request usually has a significant influence on the global sourcing management. Vendors' performance is assessed based on their ability to deal with fluctuant or urgent demand.

3.2.5　Partnership

Partnership with a supplier's, and specifically a vendor's, record of financial performance may provide grounds for a long-term relationship. If such a relationship is formed, suppliers prefer to bear more liability about product research and development. Additionally, a supplier's capability of predicting the apparel market trends may also help customers choose the right product.

3.2.6   Risk

Nowadays the global supplier selection is facing more risk factors than ever before. Many factors are affecting the global sourcing, such as political issues, social compliance and environmental sustainability, which would in turn influence the relationships between supplier and customer.

Therefore, the Multiple Criteria vendor selection problem could be described in Figure 4.1, and in general formulated as follows:

$$V = (V_1, V_2, \ldots, V_m): \text{ a set of } m \text{ vendors;}$$
$$C = (C_1, C_2, \ldots, C_n): \text{ a set of } n \text{ criteria;}$$

$A = [a_{ij}]_{mn}$: the decision matrix in which a_{ij} is the input data for vendor i associated with criterion j, $i = 1, 2, \ldots, m; j = 1, 2, \ldots, n$;

The decision matrix $A = [a_{ij}]_{mn}$ is standardized to the matrix $B = [b_{ij}]_{mn}$ using the following formula:

$$b_{ij} = \frac{a_{ij} - a_j^{min}}{a_j^{max} - a_j^{min}}, \text{ for benefit criteria;}$$

$$b_{ij} = \frac{a_j^{max} - a_{ij}}{a_j^{max} - a_j^{min}}, \text{ for cost criteria;}$$

where $a_j^{max} = \max\{a_{1j}, a_{2j}, \ldots, a_{mj}\}$, and $a_j^{min} = \min\{a_{1j}, a_{2j}, \ldots, a_{mj}\}$.

$$W = (w_1, w_2, \ldots, w_n): \text{ a set of criteria weights, and } \sum_{j=1}^{n} w_j = 1.$$

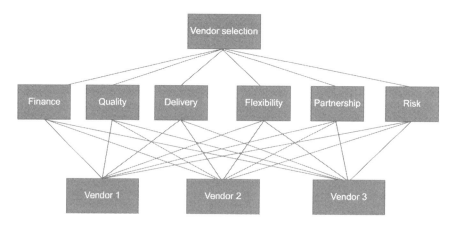

Figure 3.1 Multiple criteria vendor selection

Therefore, the overall performance with respect to a vendor could be described as:

$$S_i = \sum_{j=1}^{n} b_{ij} w_j, \, i = 1, 2, \ldots, m. \tag{3.1}$$

The decision maker chooses the vendors according to the ranking of S_i for all i. An important issue in the Multiple Criteria vendor selection problem is determining the weights w_j associated with each criterion. Although weights typically affect the results of analysis, weights determination is not easy because the definition of weights has not reached a consensus, nor are the exact values calculated by a decision maker (Wang and Luo, 2010). The existing approaches to obtaining weights can be generally divided into two sets based on the information provided, that is, subjective and objective approaches (Ma et al., 1999). More specifically, the subjective ones decide on the weights by taking into consideration of preference information of criteria offered by the managers, while the objective ones select the weights relying on the real information from decision matrix itself.

In what follows, this study provides a detailed introduction of the subjective weight determination method for vendor selection in the apparel industry. For the purpose of determining weights, some questionnaires are delivered to obtain a consensus pairwise comparison matrix $D = [d_{kj}]_{nn}$ about the criteria set C, the elements of which satisfy:

$$d_{kj} > 0, \, d_{jk} = \frac{1}{d_{kj}}, \, d_{kk} = 1, \, k, \, j = 1, 2, \ldots, n, \tag{3.2}$$

in which d_{kj} represents the corresponding weight of criterion C_k associated with criterion C_j.

The rationale of pairwise comparison matrix $D = [d_{kj}]_{nn}$ is similar to Satty's matrix (Saaty, 1977, 1980), the fundamental scale of pairwise comparisons is summarized in Table 3.3.

Table 3.3 Fundamental scale of pairwise comparisons

Scale	Description	Explanation
1	Equally important	Both elements have equal contribution to the objective
3	Medium important	Personal preference slightly prefers one entity to the other
5	Strongly important	Personal preference strongly favors one entity over the other
7	Very strongly important	Personal judgment very strongly prefers one element to the other
9	Extremely important	Personal judgment preferring one element to the other is of the largest possibility

2, 4, 6 and 8 express intermediate value

In line with Chu et al. (1979) and Ma et al. (1999), as well as regarding to the element d_{kj} of the pairwise comparison matrix $D = [d_{kj}]_{nn}$, it is preferable to determine the weight w_j so that:

$$d_{kj} \approx \frac{w_k}{w_j}. \tag{3.3}$$

Therefore, the weights could be derived by finding the optimal solutions to the following constrained optimization problem:

$$\min z = w^T F w = \sum_{k=1}^{n} \sum_{j=1}^{n} \left(d_{kj} w_j - w_k \right)^2 \tag{3.4}$$

$$s.t. \; e^T w = 1, w > 0.$$

where $e = (1, 1, \ldots, 1)^T$, $w = (w_1, w_2, \ldots, w_n)^T$ and $F = [f_{lj}]_{nn}$, and the elements of matrix F are:

$$f_{ll} = n - 2 + \sum_{k=1}^{n} d_{kl}^2, \; l = 1, 2, \ldots, n, \tag{3.5}$$

$$f_{lj} = - (d_{lj} + d_{jl}), \; l, j = 1, 2, \ldots, n, \; l \neq j. \tag{3.6}$$

Obviously, (3.4) is a non-linear programming problem. To minimize z, a Lagrangian function would be constructed as below:

$$L = w^T F w + 2\lambda (e^T w - 1), \tag{3.7}$$

where λ is the Lagrangian multiplier. The optimal solution is obtained by differentiating (3.7) with respect to w and λ, respectively. That is:

$$\begin{cases} F w + \lambda e = 0, \\ e w^T = 1, \end{cases} \tag{3.8}$$

where $0 = (0, 0, \ldots, 0)^T$.
By solving the Equation (3.8), the optimal solution to (3.4) is:

$$w^* = \frac{F^{-1} e}{e^T F^{-1} e}, \tag{3.9}$$

$$\lambda^* = \frac{-1}{e^T F^{-1} e}. \tag{3.10}$$

Because that the constraint set in (3.4) is convex, the optimal solutions (3.9) and (3.10) are global optimal.

3.3   Numerical illustration

For the purpose of demonstrating the effectiveness of the developed subjective method to determine weights associated with vendor selection criteria. A survey was conducted for the purpose of collecting required data and further evaluating

Table 3.4 Pairwise comparisons

d_{kj}	Finance	Quality	Service	Flexibility	Partnership	Risk
Finance	1	3	1/3	5	3	1/3
Quality	1/3	1	3	5	7	3
Service	3	1/3	1	9	3	1/5
Flexibility	1/5	1/5	1/9	1	1/5	1/5
Partnership	1/3	1/7	1/3	5	1	1/3
Risk	3	1/3	5	5	3	1

the preference and priority of the vendor selection criteria. This research designed a questionnaire to make pairwise comparisons between the criteria.

We launched this survey with SurveyMonkey and sent an invitation letter and the link of the questionnaire to the sourcing manager, director and EVP of apparel industry, SAC (Sustainable Apparel Coalition), Better Buying, SFBC (Sustainable Fashion Business Consortium) in January 2017. The specific respondents enabled us to realize the current situation in the apparel industry, as well as their opinions and views on vendor selection at this market state. 48 responses were collected in March 2017. The designed questionnaire can be found at this link: www.surveymonkey.com/r/NQ8JG7H.

In line with the Saaty's 1–9 scale, the qualitative judgments obtained from the pairwise comparison could effectively demonstrate the decision maker's preference among different criteria. A sufficient number of supply chain managers were invited to provide responses about the pairwise comparisons. The results received from this survey reveal the managers' judgments and priority of the criteria, which totally use the Saaty's pairwise comparison preference scale and are reported in Table 3.4.

Applying the proposed subjective weight determination method proposed in this chapter, the matrix F as (3.5) and (3.6) is reported as below:

$$F = \begin{bmatrix} 48.22 & -3.33 & -3.33 & -5.20 & -3.33 & -3.33 \\ -3.33 & 106.0 & -3.33 & -5.20 & -7.14 & -3.33 \\ -3.33 & -3.33 & 104.15 & -9.11 & -3.33 & -5.20 \\ -5.20 & -5.20 & -9.11 & 136.08 & -5.20 & -5.20 \\ -3.33 & -7.14 & -3.33 & -5.20 & 72.15 & -3.33 \\ -3.33 & -3.33 & -5.20 & -5.20 & -3.33 & 14.30 \end{bmatrix}. \tag{3.11}$$

On the strength of (3.9), the weights associated with each criterion is:

$$w = \left(w_1, w_2, w_3, w_4, w_5, w_6 \right)^T \\ = \left(0.10, 0.02, 0.02, 0.01, 0.04, 0.80 \right)^T, \tag{3.12}$$

where the subscripts 1, 2, 3, 4, 5 and 6 represent finance, quality, service, flexibility, partnership and risk, respectively. This reveals that the global sourcing

Table 3.5 Simulated data for apparel vendor selection

Vendors	Criteria					
	Finance	Quality	Service	Flexibility	Partnership	Risk
1	0.50	0.02	0.49	0.66	0.62	0.49
2	0.25	0.23	0.25	0.49	0.37	0.29
3	0.50	0.04	0.14	0.42	0.44	0.35
4	0.50	0.04	0.02	0.35	0.39	0.31
5	0.50	0.44	0.72	0.81	0.73	0.58
6	0.50	0.52	0.76	0.70	0.65	0.52
7	0.25	0.00	0.02	0.35	0.32	0.26
8	0.85	0.44	0.29	0.52	0.61	0.48
9	0.50	0.19	0.24	0.49	0.49	0.39
10	0.50	0.02	0.49	0.66	0.62	0.49

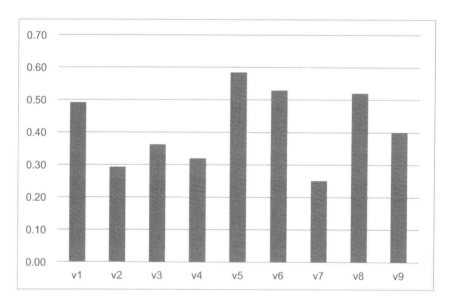

Figure 3.2 Performance of vendors

managers in apparel industry universally consider the criterion 'risk' as the most important factor. Such an observation provides managers the new insights that risk management should be paid more attention nowadays.

We now use a set of simulation data to implement the vendor selection in the apparel industry. The raw data are provided in Table 3.5.

Using the obtained weights associated with each criterion, the performance of all vendors is shown as:

$$S = (S_1, S_2, S_3, S_4, S_5, S_6, S_7, S_8, S_9, S_{10})$$
$$= (0.49, 0.29, 0.36, 0.32, 0.58, 0.53, 0.25, 0.52, 0.40),$$

which is vividly demonstrated in Figure 3.2.

The advantage of this subjective method is reflecting the subjective preference and judgment of the decision makers, as well as providing a full ranking of all vendors. However, the final results with respect to the alternative vendors could be influenced by the decision makers because the knowledge and experience may change across different decision managers.

4 Alternative objective methods for vendor selection

4.1 Introduction

The key to successful global apparel supply chain management is heavily based on the selection of qualified vendors. Simply searching vendors providing the lowest bid prices is no longer 'efficient sourcing strategy'. Multiple criteria thereby should be incorporated into the process of selecting vendors. The fundamental rationale behind this is to determine weights associated with each criterion, which play an extremely significant function in the procedure of decision making. Apart from the subjective method introduced in the previous chapter, it is also desirable to develop some eligible objective methods for the goal of determining weights in the context of Multiple Criteria vendor selection, the mechanism of which is eliciting weighting based upon the decision matrix itself. Such weights effectively eliminate decision bias and enhance the objectiveness of decision procedure (Yu and Lai, 2011). Representing objective approaches include principle element analysis, the Shannon entropy approach (Shannon, 1948; Hwang and Yoon, 1981), the coefficient of variation approach (Pomerol and Romero, 2000), multiple objective programming, CRITIC (Criteria Importance Through Intercriteria Correlation) (Diakoulaki et al., 1995), a hybrid of correlation coefficient and standard deviation logics (Wang and Luo, 2010) and others.

The Multiple Criteria vendor problem investigated in the present study could be described as follows:

$V = (V_1, V_2, \ldots, V_m)$: a set of m vendors;
$C = (C_1, C_2, \ldots, C_n)$: a set of n criteria;

$A = [a_{ij}]_{mn}$: the decision matrix in which a_{ij} is the input data for vendor i associated with criterion j, $i = 1, 2, \ldots, m$; $j = 1, 2, \ldots, n$;

The decision matrix $A = [a_{ij}]_{mn}$ is standardized to the matrix $B = [b_{ij}]_{mn}$ using the following formula:

$$b_{ij} = \frac{a_{ij} - a_j^{\min}}{a_j^{\max} - a_j^{\min}}, \text{ for benefit criteria;}$$

$$b_{ij} = \frac{a_j^{max} - a_{ij}}{a_j^{max} - a_j^{min}}, \text{ for cost criteria;}$$

where $a_j^{max} = \max\{a_{1j}, a_{2j}, \ldots, a_{mj}\}$, and $a_j^{min} = \min\{a_{1j}, a_{2j}, \ldots, a_{mj}\}$.

$W = (w_1, w_2, \ldots, w_n)$: a set of criteria weights, and $\sum_{j=1}^{n} w_j = 1$. The major purpose of such a standardization is to eliminate the influence of data magnitude.

The overall performance of a vendor is calculated as:

$$S_i = \sum_{j=1}^{n} b_{ij} w_j, \, i = 1, 2, \ldots, m. \tag{4.1}$$

Motivation of the development of objective weight determination approaches in this study is twofold. First, the proposed new approaches in this study provide more methodological choices for the supply chain managers. Second, the approaches introduced in this study enrich the theory and methodology of decision analysis.

In what follows, this study develops three objective methods for Multiple Criteria vendor selection problem using the decision criteria determined by the survey analysis in Chapter 3, that is, minimizing the overall deviation from the ideal point, minimizing the mean absolute deviation and group decision method.

4.2 The proposed methods

4.2.1 Minimizing the overall deviation from the ideal point

The rationale of minimizing the overall deviation from the ideal point approach is attempting to allow the performance with respect to each criterion as near to the ideal point as possible (Liang et al., 2008; Peng et al., 2017). This piece of research is intuitively reasonable, motivated by the observation that all vendors are always seeking to maximize the corresponding performance associated with each criterion.

This thesis transforms the normalized decision matrix $B = [b_{ij}]_{mn}$ into a weighted decision matrix $G = [g_{ij}]_{mn}$, in which

$$g_{ij} = b_{ij} w_j, \, i = 1, 2, \ldots, m, \, j = 1, 2, \ldots, n. \tag{4.2}$$

The ideal point could be formulated as $g^* = \{g_1^*, g_2^*, \ldots, g_n^*\}$, where

$$\begin{aligned} g_j^* &= \max\{g_{1j}, g_{2j}, \ldots, g_{mj}\} \\ &= \max\{b_{1j} w_j, b_{2j} w_j, \ldots, b_{mj} w_j\} \\ &= \max\{b_{1j}, b_{2j}, \ldots, b_{mj}\} w_j \\ &= b_j^* w_j, \end{aligned} \tag{4.3}$$

and b_j^*, $b_j^* = \max\{b_{1j}, b_{2j}, \ldots, b_{mj}\}$ could be regarded as the ideal point of criterion j. This definition is straightforward because the maximal value under certain criterion is reasonably taken into account as the target to reach.

With respect to each vendor i, the distance function between the real value and the ideal point under certain criterion j is defined as (Fu, Lai, Miao and Leung 2016):

$$d_{ij} = \left| b_{ij} - b_j^* \right|, \, i = 1, 2, \ldots, m, \, j = 1, 2, \ldots, n. \tag{4.4}$$

This study thereby formulates the following mathematical programming for vendor I to minimize the weighted least square of the above distance as the objective function:

$$\min z_i = \sum_{j=1}^{n} (d_{ij} w_j)^2$$

$$\text{s.t. } \sum_{j=1}^{n} w_j = 1, \tag{4.5}$$

$$w_j > 0.$$

Rational decision maker should assign a small weight w_j to a large distance d_{ij}, because the large distance indicates that it is far away from the ideal point.

At present, a multiple objective programming formulation is developed to optimize the evaluation results associated with all vendors:

$$\begin{cases} z_1 = \min \sum_{j=1}^{n} (b_{1j} - b_j^*)^2 w_j^2 \\ z_2 = \min \sum_{j=1}^{n} (b_{2j} - b_j^*)^2 w_j^2 \\ \qquad \cdots \\ z_m = \min \sum_{j=1}^{n} (b_{mj} - b_j^*)^2 w_j^2 \\ \qquad \text{s.t. } \sum_{j=1}^{n} w_j = 1. \end{cases} \tag{4.6}$$

This multiple objective programming model (4.6) could be easily transformed into a single objective programming formulation relying on the linear equal weighted summation approach (Ma et al., 1999) as:

$$\begin{cases} \min Z = \sum_{i=1}^{m} \sum_{j=1}^{n} (b_{ij} - b_j^*)^2 w_j^2 \\ \text{s.t.} \sum_{j=1}^{n} w_j = 1, w_j > 0. \end{cases} \tag{4.7}$$

In order to solve this quadratic programming model (4.7), this study constructs a Lagrangian function in terms of a Lagrange multiplier η:

$$L = \sum_{i=1}^{m} \sum_{j=1}^{n} (b_{ij} - b_j^*)^2 w_j^2 + \eta \left(\sum_{j=1}^{n} w_j - 1 \right). \tag{4.8}$$

The Hessian matrix of (4.8) of w_j is a $n \times n$ diagonal matrix, while the corresponding diagonal factors are $2\sum_{i=1}^{m}(b_{ij} - b_j^*)^2 > 0$. Hence, the Lagrangian function (4.8) definitely has a minimum value, which could be easily obtained by differentiating (4.8) associated with w_j and η respectively:

$$\begin{cases} 2\sum_{i=1}^{m}\sum_{j=1}^{n}(b_{ij} - b_j^*)^2 w_j + \eta = 0, \\ \sum_{j=1}^{n} w_j - 1 = 0. \end{cases} \tag{4.9}$$

After solving the Equation (4.9), we obtain:

$$\begin{cases} \eta^* = \dfrac{1}{2\sum_{j=1}^{n}\left[\sum_{i=1}^{m}(b_{ij} - b_j^*)^2\right]^{-1}}, \\ w_j^* = \dfrac{1}{\sum_{j=1}^{n}\left[\sum_{i=1}^{m}(b_{ij} - b_j^*)^2\right]^{-1}\sum_{i=1}^{m}(b_{ij} - b_j^*)^2}. \end{cases} \tag{4.10}$$

Due to the fact that the constraint in the Equation (4.7) is a non-empty convex set, while the objective function in the Equation (4.7) is convex as well, the optimal solutions as the Equation (4.10) are the global optimal ones.

Consequently, the performance of vendor i using the optimal weights obtained from minimizing the overall deviation from the ideal point method can be calculated as below:

$$S_i^* = \sum_{j=1}^{n} b_{ij} w_j^*, \, i = 1, 2, \ldots, m. \tag{4.11}$$

4.2.2 Minimizing the mean absolute deviation

In order to minimize the volatility of performance under different criteria, in other words, reducing the decision bias among different evaluation criteria, this study proposes the concept of mean absolute deviation and applies it to determine weights associated with each criterion. The mean absolute deviation (MAD) is defined as the arithmetic average of the absolute deviations of the inputs from the respective mean (Konno and Yamazaki, 1999). The main goal of minimizing the mean absolute deviation is to effectively reduce the decision inconsistency among various criteria, which in a manner reveals an equalitarian logic (Liang et al., 2008).

Revisit the weighted decision matrix $G = [g_{ij}]_{mn}$ in Section 4.2.1; the mean performance under certain criterion is demonstrated by $\Psi = \{\Psi_1, \Psi_2, \ldots, \Psi_n\}$, where:

$$\psi_j = \frac{\sum_{i=1}^{m} b_{ij} w_j}{m}, \, j = 1, 2, \ldots, n, \tag{4.12}$$

and $\sum\limits_{i=1}^{m} b_{ij} w_j$ is described as the mean value under criterion j.

According to Konno and Yamazaki (1999), the mean absolute deviation under certain criterion j for the weighted decision matrix $G = [g_{ij}]_{mn}$ is computed as:

$$\phi_{ij} = \left| \frac{\sum\limits_{i=1}^{m} b_{ij} w_j}{m} - b_{ij} w_j \right|, \, j = 1, 2, \dots, n. \tag{4.13}$$

Then the overall mean absolute deviation with respect to vendor i, $i = 1$, $2, \dots, m$ could be reasonably calculated as

$$\phi_i = \sum\limits_{j=1}^{n} \left| \frac{\sum\limits_{i=1}^{m} b_{ij}}{m} - b_{ij} \right| w_j. \tag{4.14}$$

Motivated by Wang and Wang (2013), it is then preferable to determine weights to expect the total mean absolute deviation associated with all vendors as small as possible. Similar to Section 4.2.1, this suggests this study to propose the following multiple objective quadratic programming model for determining the criteria weights for vendor selection:

$$
\begin{cases}
f_1 = \min \sum\limits_{j=1}^{n} \left(\frac{\sum\limits_{i=1}^{m} b_{ij}}{m} - b_{1j} \right)^2 w_j^2 \\[4ex]
f_2 = \min \sum\limits_{j=1}^{n} \left(\frac{\sum\limits_{i=1}^{m} b_{ij}}{m} - b_{2j} \right)^2 w_j^2 \\[4ex]
\quad \dots \\[2ex]
f_m = \min \sum\limits_{j=1}^{n} \left(\frac{\sum\limits_{i=1}^{m} b_{ij}}{m} - b_{mj} \right)^2 w_j^2 \\[4ex]
\quad s.t. \sum\limits_{j=1}^{n} w_j = 1.
\end{cases}
\tag{4.15}
$$

This is the other Lagrangian function by introducing a Lagrange multiplier λ:

$$LL = \sum\limits_{i=1}^{m} \sum\limits_{j=1}^{n} \left(\frac{\sum\limits_{i=1}^{m} b_{ij}}{m} - b_{ij} \right)^2 w_j^2 + \lambda \left(\sum\limits_{j=1}^{n} w_j - 1 \right). \tag{4.16}$$

The Hessian matrix of (4.16) of w_j is a $n \times n$ diagonal matrix while the respective

diagonal factors are $2\left(\dfrac{\sum_{i=1}^{m} b_{ij}}{m} - b_{ij}\right)^2$. Therefore, the Lagrangian function LL as

the Equation (4.16) has a minimum value, which could be effectively computed in terms of differentiating (4.16) associated with w_j and λ, respectively:

$$\begin{cases} 2\sum_{i=1}^{m}\sum_{j=1}^{n}\left(\dfrac{\sum_{i=1}^{m} b_{ij}}{m} - b_{ij}\right)^2 w_j + \lambda = 0, \\ \sum_{j=1}^{n} w_j - 1 = 0. \end{cases} \tag{4.17}$$

Solving the Equation (4.17), we obtain

$$\begin{cases} \lambda^* = \dfrac{1}{2\sum_{j=1}^{n}\left[\sum_{i=1}^{m}\left(\dfrac{\sum_{i=1}^{m} b_{ij}}{m} - b_{ij}\right)^2\right]^{-1}}, \\ w_j^* = \dfrac{1}{\sum_{j=1}^{n}\left[\sum_{i=1}^{m}\left(\dfrac{\sum_{i=1}^{m} b_{ij}}{m} - b_{ij}\right)^2\right]^{-1} \sum_{i=1}^{m}\left(\dfrac{\sum_{i=1}^{m} b_{ij}}{m} - b_{ij}\right)^2}. \end{cases} \tag{4.18}$$

Similarly, these are the global optimal solutions.

Once again, the performance of vendor i using the optimal weights derived from minimizing the mean absolute deviation method can be reasonably calculated as below:

$$S_i^* = \sum_{j=1}^{n} b_{ij} w_j^*, \ i = 1, 2, \ldots, m. \tag{4.19}$$

4.2.3   *Group decision*

In the context of Multiple Criteria vendor selection determined by a committee, it will be extremely hard to achieve a group consensus on the weighting schemes considering multiple evaluation criteria. However, achieving a widely accepted group consensus according to different preferences and judgments provided by distinct stakeholders remains an unresolved task in the existing literature (Yu and Lai, 2011). This inspires a set of active research on Group Decision Making (GDM) methodology development and practical application (Beynon, 2005).

Table 4.1 The general form of GDM

Alternatives	DM_1			...	DM_K		
	C_1	... C_n	$C_1, ..., C_n$		C_1	... C_n	
A_1	$U_1(A_1, C_1)$	... $U_1(A_1, C_n)$	...		$U_K(A_1, C_1)$	... $U_K(A_1, C_n)$	
...	...	... ...	...		...	... ...	
A_1	$U_1(A_1, C_1)$	... $U_1(A_1, C_n)$	...		$U_K(A_1, C_1)$	... $U_K(A_1, C_n)$	

The main procedures of Multiple Criteria GDM method are presented as below (Yu and Lai, 2011):

1   identifying group members/decision makers;
2   implementing general MCDM procedure for single stakeholder; and
3   formulating of group consensus.

Therefore, a general description of Multiple Criteria vendor selection problem using GDM is denoted in Table 4.1.

In this study, for the ease of demonstrating the mechanism of group decision making, different decision makers are identified by weight determination approaches, namely the coefficient of variation approach, the Shannon entropy approach, and distance-based approach, the steps of which would be introduced as follows. Then a consensus model is proposed to reduce the discrepancy among different stakeholders.

Recall the general form of Multiple Criteria vendor selection problem in global sourcing previously presented:

$V = (V_1, V_2, \ldots, V_m)$: a set of m vendors;
$C = (C_1, C_2, \ldots, C_n)$: a set of n criteria;

$A = [a_{ij}]_{mn}$: the decision matrix in which a_{ij} is the input data for vendor i associated with criterion j, $i = 1, 2, \ldots, m; j = 1, 2, \ldots, n;$

The decision matrix $A = [a_{ij}]_{mn}$ is standardized to the matrix $B = [b_{ij}]_{mn}$ using the following formula:

$$b_{ij} = \frac{a_{ij} - a_j^{min}}{a_j^{max} - a_j^{min}}, \text{ for benefit criteria;}$$

$$b_{ij} = \frac{a_j^{max} - a_{ij}}{a_j^{max} - a_j^{min}}, \text{ for cost criteria;}$$

where $a_j^{max} = \max\{a_{1j}, a_{2j}, \ldots, a_{mj}\}$, and $a_j^{min} = \min\{a_{1j}, a_{2j}, \ldots, a_{mj}\}$.

$W = (w_1, w_2, \ldots, w_n)$: a set of criteria weights, and $\sum_{j=1}^{n} w_j = 1$.

The overall performance with respect to a vendor could be described as:

$$S_i = \sum_{j=1}^{n} b_{ij} w_j, i = 1, 2, \ldots, m.$$

Approach 1: Coefficient of variation

Step 1: Mean computation of the normalized matrix $B = [b_{ij}]_{mn}$.

Regarding to evaluation criterion j, the mean value could be obtained by the following expression:

$$\bar{b}_j = \frac{1}{m} \sum_{i=1}^{m} b_{ij}, j = 1, 2, \ldots, n. \tag{4.20}$$

Step 2: Standard deviation computation of the normalized matrix $B = [b_{ij}]_{mn}$.

Using the mean value in Equation (4.20) and the input data in $B = [b_{ij}]_{mn}$, the standard deviation can be computed by:

$$\sigma_j = \sqrt{\frac{1}{m} \sum_{i=1}^{m} \left(\bar{b}_j - b_{ij} \right)^2}, j = 1, 2, \ldots, n. \tag{4.21}$$

Step 3: Coefficient of variation computation.

Employing the above mean and standard deviation computations, the coefficient of variation is denoted as:

$$\delta_j = \frac{\sigma_j}{\bar{b}_j}, j = 1, 2, \ldots, n. \tag{4.22}$$

This coefficient of variation could typically be regarded as a dispersion measurement. That is, the larger the coefficient of variation, the higher the dispersion degree.

Step 4: Criteria weights determination.

Regarding each evaluation criterion, the corresponding weight can be determined by:

$$w_j = \frac{\delta_j}{\sum_{j=1}^{n} \delta_j}, j = 1, 2, \ldots, n. \tag{4.23}$$

Approach 2: Shannon entropy

Entropy concept is proposed by Shannon (1948) and in general plays a fundamental role in information theory, and it is well-known as a useful and effective mathematical tool to measure importance degrees. Employing Shannon entropy to measure the importance degree is pioneered by Zeleny (1982) in the circumstance of MCDM. In line with the work of Soleimani-damaneh and Zarepisheh (2009), we introduce the following three steps to decide on the criteria weights on the basis of Shannon entropy.

Step 1: Entropy calculation.

For each evaluation criterion j, $j = 1, 2, \ldots, n$, the entropy could be computed as

$$f_j = -[\ln(m)]^{-1} \sum_{i=1}^{m} b_{ij} \ln(b_{ij}), \ j = 1, 2, \ldots, n. \tag{4.24}$$

Step 2: Discriminability computation.

For each criterion j, $j = 1, 2, \ldots, n$, the degree of discriminability could be computed as:

$$k_j = 1 - f_j, \ j = 1, 2, \ldots, n. \tag{4.25}$$

Step 3: Criteria weights determination.

For each evaluation criterion j, $j = 1, 2, \ldots, n$, the corresponding weight could be elicited as:

$$w_j = \frac{k_j}{\sum_{j=1}^{n} k_j}, \ j = 1, 2, \ldots, n. \tag{4.26}$$

Approach 3: Distance-based approach

Step 1: Determination of optimistic and pessimistic elements for the j th criterion.

For the j th criterion, optimistic and pessimistic elements are defined as:

Optimistic elements: $V^+ = (V_1^+, V_2^+, \ldots, V_n^+)$;

Pessimistic elements: $V^- = (V_1^-, V_2^-, \ldots, V_n^-)$,

where $V_j^+ = \max_{i=1,2,\ldots,m} \{b_{ij}\}$, $V_j^- = \max_{i=1, 2, \ldots, m} \{b_{ij}\}$, $j = 1, 2, \ldots, n$.

Step 2: Distance computation between the optimistic and the pessimistic elements.

Considering optimistic and pessimistic elements, the distance between elements of the j th criterion and the optimistic/pessimistic elements of the j th criterion can be computed as:

$$D_j^+ = \sqrt{\sum_{i=1}^{m}(b_{ij} - V_j^+)^2};$$

$$D_j^- = \sqrt{\sum_{i=1}^{m}(b_{ij} - V_j^-)^2}. \tag{4.27}$$

Step 3: Dispersion measurement for each criterion

As for the proposed distance-based method in this study, the measurement of dispersion for the j th criterion is described as $\lambda_j = \dfrac{D_j^+}{D_j^+ + D_j^-}$, $j = 1,$ $2, \ldots, n$. The larger the value of λ_j is, the dispersion measurement and accordingly the more important is the j th criterion.

Step 4: Criteria weights determination.

Regarding to each criterion j, $j = 1, 2, \ldots, n$, the relative weights can be effectively determined using the dispersion measurement derived from the previous step, that is,

$$w_j = \frac{\lambda_j}{\sum\limits_{j=1}^{n} \lambda_j}, \quad j = 1, 2, \ldots, n. \tag{4.28}$$

On the strength of these weights derived from each decision maker, alternatively represented by the above three approaches, different evaluation results about the Multiple Criteria vendor selection problem would be inevitably obtained. Without loss of generality, we summarize the assessment results collected from distinct decision makers and then formulate the following decision matrix:

$$S_{mK} = \begin{bmatrix} S_{11} & S_{12} & \cdots & S_{1K} \\ S_{21} & S_{22} & \cdots & S_{2K} \\ \cdots & \cdots & \cdots & \cdots \\ S_{m1} & S_{m2} & \cdots & S_{mK} \end{bmatrix}, \tag{4.29}$$

the row of which is related to vendors, while the column of which is about different decision makers.

Regarding each vendor, we propose the definition of peer-evaluation performance as follows.

Definition 4.1: With respect to each vendor i, $i = 1, 2, \ldots, m$, the peer-assessment performance could be described as the average of the results obtained from different decision makers, that is, $S_i = \dfrac{S_{i1} + S_{i2} + \cdots + S_{iK}}{K}$, $i = 1, 2, \ldots, m$.

Similarly, the input data in the matrix (4.29) could be reasonably recognized as the self-assessment performance. The mentioned twin definitions, namely, the peer-assessment and the self-assessment, are actually inspired from the cross-efficiency aggregation in Data Envelopment Analysis (Wu et al., 2012).

Euclidean distance is employed here to denote the value of discrepancy between the self-assessment and the peer-assessment performance (Yu and Lai,

2011; Cao et al., 2016). The so-called discrepancy in this study could be recognized as the noisy or information redundancy produced from evaluation procedure, which of course would be decreased or excluded for the purpose of obtaining reasonable evaluation result with respect to each vendor (Shannon, 1948). In general, the smaller the aforementioned distance is, the more reliable the assessment between results of the self-assessment and the peer-assessment performance, and the better the final assessment outcomes.

> **Definition 4.2**: With respect to every vendor i, $i = 1, 2, \ldots, m$, the aforementioned distance function between the self-assessment and peer-assessment performance is defined as:

$$d_{ik} = |\, S_{ik} - S_i\,|, \; k = 1, 2, \ldots, K. \tag{4.30}$$

Based upon this distance function, we propose a mathematical programming model that uses the weighted least square of this distance as the objective function:

$$\min z_i = \sum_{k=1}^{K} (d_{ik}\lambda_k)^2$$

$$\text{s.t. } \sum_{k=1}^{K} \lambda_k = 1, \lambda_k > 0. \tag{4.31}$$

The rationale behind this mathematical programming model is assigning a relative small weight to the large distance value.

Because of the vendor selection process, this study formulates the following multiple objective programming model considering all vendors to maximize the performance associated with all vendors:

$$\left\{ \begin{array}{l} \begin{cases} \min z_1 = \sum_{k=1}^{K} (d_{1k}\lambda_k)^2 \\[4pt] \min z_2 = \sum_{k=1}^{K} (d_{2k}\lambda_k)^2 \\[4pt] \qquad \cdots \\[4pt] \min z_m = \sum_{k=1}^{K} (d_{mk}\lambda_k)^2 \end{cases} \\[6pt] \text{s.t. } \sum_{k=1}^{K} \lambda_k = 1, \lambda_k > 0. \end{array} \right. \tag{4.32}$$

The expression (4.32) could be converted from a multiple objective programming model into a single objective programming model using the linear equal weighted summation approach (Ma et al., 1999), that is:

$$\left| \begin{array}{l} \min Z = \sum_{i=1}^{m} \sum_{k=1}^{K} d_{ik}^2 \lambda_k^2 \\[4pt] \text{s.t. } \sum_{k=1}^{K} \lambda_k = 1, \lambda_k > 0. \end{array} \right. \tag{4.33}$$

By introducing a Lagrange multiplier η, the following Lagrangian function is proposed to determine the optimal λ_k:

$$L = \sum_{i=1}^{m} \sum_{k=1}^{K} d_{ik}^2 \lambda_k^2 + \eta \left(\sum_{k=1}^{K} \lambda_k - 1 \right),$$
(4.34)

The Hessian matrix of this Lagrangian function (4.34) with respect to λ_k is:

$$H = \begin{vmatrix} \dfrac{\partial^2 L}{\partial \lambda_1^2} & \dfrac{\partial^2 L}{\partial \lambda_1 \partial \lambda_2} & \cdots & \dfrac{\partial^2 L}{\partial \lambda_1 \partial \lambda_K} \\[2mm] \dfrac{\partial^2 L}{\partial \lambda_2 \partial \lambda_1} & \dfrac{\partial^2 L}{\partial \lambda_2^2} & \cdots & \dfrac{\partial^2 L}{\partial \lambda_2 \partial \lambda_K} \\[2mm] \cdots & \cdots & \cdots & \cdots \\[2mm] \dfrac{\partial^2 L}{\partial \lambda_K \partial \lambda_1} & \dfrac{\partial^2 L}{\partial \lambda_K \partial \lambda_2} & \cdots & \dfrac{\partial^2 L}{\partial \lambda_K^2} \end{vmatrix},$$
(4.35)

in which $\dfrac{\partial^2 L}{\partial \lambda_k \partial \lambda_l} = 0, \, k \neq l, \dfrac{\partial^2 L}{\partial \lambda_k^2} = 2 \sum_{i=1}^{m} \sum_{k=1}^{K} d_{ik}^2 > 0.$

Based on the Hessian theorem, the developed Lagrangian function (4.34) definitely has the minimum value, which could be obtained by setting:

$$\begin{cases} \dfrac{\partial L}{\partial \eta} = 0, \\[3mm] \dfrac{\partial L}{\partial \lambda_k} = 0, \end{cases}$$
(4.36)

and thereby the optimal solutions are:

$$\begin{cases} \eta = \dfrac{1}{2 \sum_{k=1}^{K} \left(\sum_{i=1}^{m} d_{ik}^2 \right)^{-1}} \\[5mm] \lambda_k^* = \dfrac{1}{\left[\sum_{k=1}^{K} \left(\sum_{i=1}^{m} d_{ik}^2 \right)^{-1} \right] \left[\sum_{i=1}^{m} d_{ik}^2 \right]} \end{cases}$$
(4.37)

If we revisit the Lagrangian function (4.34), we find that the constraints of it are non-empty convex sets, and the objective function is convex. Therefore, function (4.34) is a convex programming formulation, and then the obtained $\lambda_k^*, \, k = 1, 2, \ldots, K$ are surely the global optimal solutions to (4.34).

Finally, the performance for each vendor $i, \, i = 1, 2, \ldots, m$ could be obtained using this group decision making method as:

$$S_i^* = \sum_{k=1}^{K} \lambda_k^* S_{ik}, \, i = 1, 2, \ldots, m.$$
(4.38)

4.3 Case study

For the purpose of illustrating the effectiveness of these methods in the process of Multiple Criteria vendor selection in global sourcing, this chapter uses the evaluation criteria verified by the empirical study performed in the previous chapter, that are finance, quality, service, flexibility, partnership and risk. Once again, this chapter uses another set of simulation data reported in Table 4.2 to demonstrate the analysis.

This chapter first test the effectiveness of two methods that minimize the total deviation from the ideal point (TDIP) and the mean absolute deviation (MAD), and then compare the results obtained according to them, respectively. Such analysis is conducted because these two objective weights determination methods could be recognized as the decisions made by a single decision maker, which are different with the forthcoming group decision making. According to the expressions of (4.10) and (4.18), the common weights associated with each evaluation criterion are:

$$
\begin{aligned}
w_{TDIP} &= (0.17, 0.12, 0.15, 0.35, 0.09, 0.11), \\
w_{MAD} &= (0.18, 0.15, 0.20, 0.23, 0.11, 0.13).
\end{aligned}
\tag{4.39}
$$

Using the weights listed in (4.39), the scores and rankings with respect to each vendor are presented in Table 4.3 and Figure 4.1.

Although the results derived according to both, minimizing the total deviation from the ideal point and the mean absolute deviation are mildly different, the final ranking among ten vendors is robust:

$$
v6 \succ v3 \succ v7 \succ v10 \succ v4 \succ v8 \succ v9 \succ v5 \succ v1 \succ v2 .
$$

Next, we use the simulated data in Table 4.3 to show the effectiveness of the developed group decision-making approach. According to the weights

Table 4.2 Simulated data for apparel vendor selection

Vendors	Criteria					
	Finance	Quality	Service	Flexibility	Partnership	Risk
1	0.05	0.05	0.04	0.04	0.04	0.04
2	0.04	0.04	0.04	0.04	0.04	0.04
3	0.09	0.09	0.07	0.07	0.08	0.08
4	0.06	0.06	0.07	0.07	0.07	0.07
5	0.04	0.04	0.05	0.05	0.04	0.04
6	0.10	0.10	0.07	0.07	0.10	0.10
7	0.09	0.08	0.09	0.08	0.04	0.04
8	0.08	0.09	0.04	0.04	0.09	0.08
9	0.06	0.05	0.06	0.06	0.04	0.04
10	0.06	0.06	0.07	0.07	0.08	0.08

Table 4.3 Results from TDIP and MAD

Vendors	TDIP		MAD	
	Scores	Ranking	Scores	Ranking
1	0.0648	9	0.0650	9
2	0.0616	10	0.0614	10
3	0.1296	2	0.1299	2
4	0.1098	5	0.1081	5
5	0.0748	8	0.0730	8
6	0.1408	1	0.1432	1
7	0.1196	3	0.1179	3
8	0.0969	6	0.1023	6
9	0.0864	7	0.0845	7
10	0.1160	4	0.1147	4

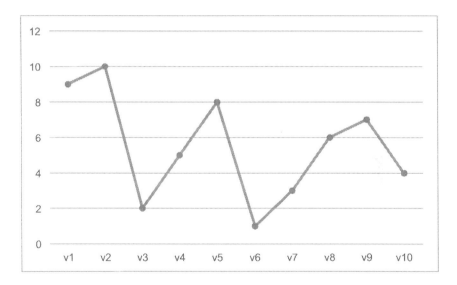

Figure 4.1 Ranking of vendors

determination approaches, including the coefficient of variation (1), the Shannon entropy (2) and distance-based (3), three sets of common weights associated with the evaluation criteria (finance, quality, service, flexibility, partnership and risk) in global sourcing are:

$$w_1 = (0.16, 0.17, 0.15, 0.14, 0.20, 0.18),$$
$$w_2 = (0.15, 0.17, 0.13, 0.12, 0.23, 0.20),$$
$$w_3 = (0.16, 0.17, 0.17, 0.14, 0.18, 0.18),$$

(4.40)

Table 4.4 Vendor selection using group decision-making method

Vendors	Coefficient of variation		Shannon entropy		Distance		Group decision	
	Scores	Ranking	Scores	Ranking	Scores	Ranking	Scores	Ranking
1	0.0651	9	0.0651	9	0.0651	9	0.0651	9
2	0.0613	10	0.0614	10	0.0613	10	0.0613	10
3	0.1302	2	0.1302	2	0.1302	2	0.1302	2
4	0.1072	6	0.1073	5	0.1073	6	0.1072	6
5	0.0697	8	0.0689	8	0.0703	8	0.0697	8
6	0.1488	1	0.1504	1	0.1479	1	0.1489	1
7	0.1077	5	0.1045	6	0.1098	5	0.1077	5
8	0.1137	4	0.1167	4	0.1117	4	0.1137	4
9	0.0796	7	0.0783	7	0.0805	7	0.0796	7
10	0.1165	3	0.1174	3	0.1160	3	0.1165	3

The performance with respect to each vendor based on the weights in (4.40) could be reasonably regarded as the results determined by a single decision maker. In line with the group decision-making framework developed in this study, the set of weights for aggregating different decision makers' results are derived using the Expression (4.37), that is

$$(\lambda_1, \lambda_2, \lambda_3) = (0.9611, 0.0168, 0.0222). \tag{4.41}$$

This set of common weights shows that the results obtained from group decision-making method are heavily dependent on that of the coefficient of variation approach ($\lambda_1 = 0.9611$). Therefore, the Multiple Criteria vendor selection problem using the group decision-making method could be determined, which is reported in Table 4.4.

Obviously, the evaluation results among the ten vendors determined by different decision makers are different, because different weights have been assigned to each criterion. More specifically, the ranking of the coefficient of variation and the distance-based approach is:

$$v6 \succ v3 \succ v10 \succ v8 \succ v7 \succ v4 \succ v9 \succ v5 \succ v1 \succ v2, \tag{4.42}$$

that of Shannon entropy is:

$$v6 \succ v3 \succ v10 \succ v8 \succ v4 \succ v7 \succ v9 \succ v5 \succ v1 \succ v2. \tag{4.43}$$

Furthermore, as shown in Figure 4.2, the ranking positions of vendor 1, vendor 2, vendor 3, vendor 5, vendor 6, vendor 8, vendor 9 and vendor 10 are the same across the results obtained by a single decision maker and a group decision.

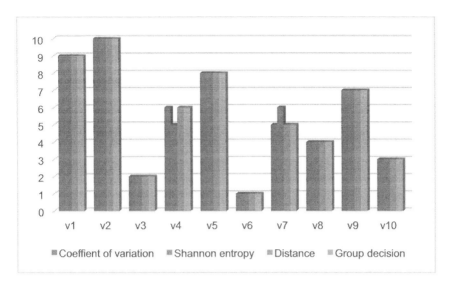

Figure 4.2 Ranking of vendors using group decision-making method

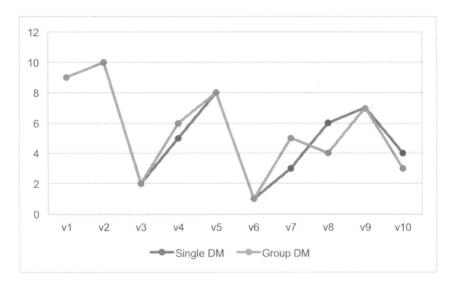

Figure 4.3 Comparisons between single and group decision making

This reveals that their ranking positions are extremely robust and reliable in the evaluation process. Only that of vendor 4 and vendor 7 are different, caused by the Shannon entropy approach.

Consequently, the evaluation results derived from different objective methods, including minimizing the total deviation from the ideal point, minimizing the mean absolute deviation, and the group decision-making method, are compared in Figure 4.3. The first two are categorized as the result determined by a single decision maker.

Figure 4.3 indicates that the results obtained from the individual decision maker and group decision making are the same for vendor 1, vendor 2, vendor 3, vendor 5, vendor 6 and vendor 9, and the rest of them are mildly different. The largest difference arises from vendor 7 and vendor 8.

Based on all the above analysis from the objective analysis, the results of vendor 1, vendor 2, vendor 3, vendor 5, vendor 6 and vendor 9 are significantly robust because all proposed objective methods in this study generate the same ranking positions for them.

4.4   Discussion

Based on the evaluation criteria for vendor selection in global sourcing determined in the previous chapter, this chapter proposes the following objective weights determination methods:

1   minimizing the total deviation from the ideal point;
2   minimizing the mean absolute deviation;
3   group decision making, in which individual decision makers are identified by coefficient of variation approach, Shannon entropy approach and distance-based approach.

The analysis in this study not only shows the robustness, but also the effectiveness of the proposed methods in terms of providing a complete ranking of the vendors. However, although these objective methods determine the weights using the data set itself and some mathematical models, they inevitably ignore the decision makers' subjective judgments on the problem. For ease of demonstrating, this study only uses three approaches to represent three single decision makers. However, future research should incorporate industry managers' experiences to develop more appropriate approaches to denote different decision makers.

5 Vendor selection under uncertain preference among evaluation criteria

5.1 Introduction

In the context of global sourcing, vendor selection is playing an extremely significant role to achieve the strategic goals of supply chain management (Kumar et al., 2004, 2006). In recent years, how to determine a set of qualified vendors in the supply chain has turned out to be a key strategic consideration (Chen et al., 2006). Choosing the right vendor is a critical decision, with various managerial implications in the context of supply chain management. The vendor selection problem is a complicated issue because of several reasons. In essence, the vendor selection problem could be recognized as a MCDM problem that uses imprecise and uncertain data (Yang et al., 2008). This is because of the fact that the Multiple Criteria vendor selection problem usually proceeds considering both intangible and tangible evaluation factors (Demitras and Üstün, 2008). Therefore, crisp data are inappropriate to model some practical situations.

In such uncertain decision-making situations, fuzzy theory has been performing as a useful method for dealing with these uncertain factors in the literature of vendor selection. Kumar et al. (2004) formulate a fuzzy mixed integer vendor selection framework with various main goals: the total rejections, minimizing the overall cost and the belated deliveries. Haq and Kannan (2006) use the fuzzy analytical hierarchy process (AHP) based on an empirical study to develop a structural model to implement vendor selection. Bayrak et al. (2007) employ a fuzzy vendor selection mechanism to completely rank the technically efficient vendors. Amid et al. (2006) develop a fuzzy multi-objective linear programming method to handle the imprecise information and uncertainties of the goals, constraints and parameters. Yang et al. (2008) propose a combined fuzzy MCDM method for handling vendor selection. Ordoobadi (2009) applies fuzzy logic allowing the decision makers to describe uncertain information in linguistic manners. Kuo et al. (2010) integrate fuzzy AHP and fuzzy dDEA to support vendor selection, and demonstrate the practical application of this method in a Taiwanese auto lighting system company in Taiwan. Sevkli (2010) propose a new method, namely, the fuzzy ELECTRE (ELimination Et Choix Traduisant la REalité) for supplier selection, which is applied in a manufacturing company in Turkey. Amin et al. (2011) develop and apply the fuzzy SWOT analysis to choose proper vendors.

Amid et al. (2011) employ the fuzzy set theory in the presence of uncertain input data and develop a weighted max–min fuzzy approach to fix the uncertainty as well as different weights with respect to evaluation criteria.

Different from the previous work for handling the uncertainties in the Multiple Criteria vendor selection problem, the primary purpose of this study is using interval values to denote the uncertainties here, and then employ a stochastic multicriteria acceptability analysis (SMAA-2) (Lahdelma et al., 1998; Lahdelma and Salminen, 2001) to provide a full rank of vendors. The aforementioned decision matrix with interval data is typically regarded as a stochastic optimization problem. Besides these, SMAA-2 is introduced, along with the concepts of rank acceptability index, confidence factor and central weight vector.

The main contribution of this research is summarized below. First, the supplier selection problem with interval values is deemed a stochastic optimization problem. Second, SMAA-2 is introduced, along with the concepts of rank acceptability index, confidence factor and central weight vector. Third, we apply SMAA-2 to the supplier selection problem with interval data and propose a holistic rank of the candidate suppliers. Even though the classical supplier selection problem has been largely explored in literature, such investigation in this study is completely new and of both academic and practical significances and values.

5.2 Vendor selection under uncertain preference among evaluation criteria

Recall the Multiple Criteria vendor selection problem with uncertain input data as below:

$V = (V_1, V_2, \ldots , V_m)$: a set of m vendors.
$C = (C_1, C_2, \ldots , C_n)$: a set of n criteria.

$A = \left[\left[\underline{a}_{ij}, \bar{a}_{ij}\right]\right]_{mn}$: the decision matrix where $\underline{a}_{ij}$ and $\bar{a}_{ij}$ are the lower and upper bounds of the certain input aij for vendor i associated with criterion j, i = 1, 2, . . . , m; j = 1, 2, . . . , n. In general, the precise data in the decision matrix imply $\underline{a}_{ij} = \bar{a}_{ij}$.

In line with the statement from Yang et al. (2012), this decision matrix $A = \left[\left[\underline{a}_{ij}, \bar{a}_{ij}\right]\right]_{mn}$ could be recognized as a stochastic MCDM problem. In what follows, this study briefly reviews the SMAA-2 approach developed by Lahdelma and Salminen (2001), which effectively solves these series of stochastic Multiple Criteria decision-making problems through providing a holistic rank of all alternatives.

5.3 Stochastic Multicriteria Acceptability Analysis (SMAA)

SMAA denotes a collection of approaches to supporting MCDM problems involving inexact, unknown or in part uncertain inputs. The logic with respect to SMAA is discovering the weight set to determine the preference degrees that make all alternatives achieve the corresponding most-favored position, or guarantee a specified rank for a certain alternative. Lahdelma et al. (1998) pioneered the discovery of this research and developed rank acceptability index, confidence factor and central weight vector with respect to all alternatives. Then, Lahdelma and Salminen (2001) further give an extension of the first version of SMAA through taking into account all possible ranks, presenting a holistic SMAA-2 analysis to vividly determine comprehensive ranking of all alternatives.

5.3.1 Preliminaries

Being consistent with the decision matrix $A = \left[\left[\underline{a}_{ij}, \bar{a}_{ij} \right] \right]_{mn}$ with uncertain data, we consider that neither expert-specific evaluation data nor weights are clearly known. This research assumes that the preference information of a decision maker across all experts' evaluations could be denoted through a utility function $g(i, w), i = \{1, 2, \ldots, m\}$, where the weight vector w is constructed to quantitatively reflect the subjective preference knowledge across experts' judgments. Moreover, the uncertain evaluation values from experts on suppliers are denoted through stochastic variables ξ_{ij} using stipulated or estimated density function $f(\xi)$ that distributed in the decision space $X \subseteq \Re^{m \times n}$. Moreover, the imprecise weight vector could be denoted by a weight distribution with density function and is described by:

$$W = \left\{ w \subseteq \Re^n : \sum_{j=1}^{n} w_j = 1, w_j \geq 0 \right\}. \tag{5.1}$$

Total absence of weight vector knowledge could be described in a 'Bayesian' manner considering a uniform weight distribution in space W, such as,
$$f(w) = \frac{1}{Vol(W)} = \frac{(n-1)!}{\sqrt{n}}.$$
Based upon the above descriptions, the utility function is thereby employed to map the stochastic experts' evaluation values and weight distributions into utility distributions $g(\xi_i, w)$.

This research uses a ranking-based expression indicating the ranking position of an individual supplier as an integer starting from the best ranking position ($=1$) to the worst ranking position ($=m$) as follows:

$$rank\,(\xi_i, w) = 1 + \sum_l \rho(g(\xi_l, w) > g(\xi_i, w)), \tag{5.2}$$

in which ρ (true) $= 1$ and ρ (false) $= 0$.

The proposed SMAA-2 approach is completely based upon investigating the sets of preferable rank weights $W_i^r(\xi)$ that are denoted as:

$$W_i^r(\xi) = \left\{ w \in W : rank(\xi_i, w) = r \right\}, \tag{5.3}$$

in which a weight $w \in W_i^r(\xi)$ grants that alternative ξ_i achieves the specific rank position r.

5.3.2   Useful indices

This subsection introduces several useful indices proposed by SMAA-2 method. The first index is the rank acceptability index b_i^r, which could be explained as the expected scale of the group of preferable rank weights. In details, b_i^r quantifies the categories of distinct values that guarantee alternative ξ_i achieve ranking position r, and can be computed using:

$$b_i^r = \int_X f(\xi) \int_{W_i^r(\xi)} f(w)\,dw\,d\xi \tag{5.4}$$

Undoubtedly, the rank acceptability index b_i^r distributes in the interval $[0, 1]$, and $b_i^r = 0$ demonstrates that the alternative ξ_i never reaches ranking position r, while $b_i^r = 1$ represents that the alternative ξ_i always obtains ranking position r, neglecting the influence of the choice with respect to weights. Furthermore, the rank acceptability index could be utilized in the Multiple Criteria alternatives assessment. With respect to large-scale problems, it is reasonable propose an iterative process, wherein the k best ranks (kbr) acceptabilities are performed at every interaction k:

$$a_i^k = \sum_{r=1}^{k} b_i^r \tag{5.5}$$

The kbr-acceptability a_i^k is deemed as a description of the status of different preferences that assure alternative ξ_i any of the k best ranking position. Such a process will be completed in the case of at least one alternative obtaining an eligible multitude of the weights.

The aforementioned weight space associated the k best ranking position with respect to an alternative is reasonably denoted using the idea of central kbr weight vector w_i^k as follows:

$$w_i^k = \int_X f(\xi) \sum_{r=1}^{k} \int_{W_i^r(\xi)} f(w)\,w\,dw\,d\xi \, / \, a_i^k \tag{5.6}$$

Taking the certain weight distribution into consideration, the central kbr weight vector is known as the best single vector description considering the preferences of an individual decision maker who gives an alternative, possibly ranking all positions from 1 to k.

The third index is defined as the nbr confidence factor p_i^k, which is reasonably described as the possibility that one alternative obtains any ranking position from 1 to k in the case of the central kbr weight vector is derived and calculated by:

$$p_i^k = \int_{\xi:rank(\xi_i,w_i^k)} f(\xi)\,d\xi \tag{5.7}$$

Further detailed information on the above three indices could be obtained in the research paper by Lahdelma and Salminen (2001). An introduction about applying SMAA is presented by Tervonen and Lahdelma (2007).

5.3.3 *Holistic evaluation of rank acceptabilities*

Based upon the aforementioned rank acceptabilities, the next step is to propose an auxiliary approach to incorporating the rank acceptabilities into holistic acceptability indices for all alternatives as below:

$$a_i^h = \sum_{r=1}^{m} \alpha^r b_i^r, \tag{5.8}$$

where α^r could be known as metaweights to construct holistic acceptability indices and meet the following order: $1 = \alpha^1 \geq \alpha^2 \geq \ldots \geq \alpha^m \geq 0$.

The elicitation of so-called metaweights is in a sense a weight determination process with respect to a lexicographic decision problem, which typically assigns the biggest amount to $\alpha 1$, and the smallest amount to αm. Regarding assigning weights to ranks, Barron and Barrett (1996) develop several effective and efficacious methods, including the rank-sum method, i.e.: $\alpha^r(RS) = \dfrac{2(m+1-r)}{m(m+1)}, r = 1, 2, \ldots, m,$ reciprocal of the ranks method, i.e., $\alpha^r(RR) = \dfrac{1/r}{\sum_{r=1}^{m} 1/r}, r = 1, 2, \ldots, m$, and rank-order centroid method, i.e., $\alpha^r(ROC) = \dfrac{1}{m}\sum_{r=1}^{m}\dfrac{1}{r}, r = 1, 2, \ldots, m$. This study uses ROC to decide on $\alpha r, r = 1, 2, \ldots, m$, since this has been claimed as more straightforward, accurate and efficacious, and it is capable of providing a reasonable implementation procedure (Barron and Barrett, 1996).

The holistic evaluation of rank acceptability indices generates an overall assessment of the acceptability of all alternatives. This is helpful to effectively rank and sort alternatives.

5.4 Numerical study

For the purpose of verifying the usage and effectiveness of applying the SMAA-2 to solve the Multiple Criteria vendor selection problem consider six criteria, namely finance, quality, service, flexibility, partnership and risk. The interval values associated with these criteria are simulated as Table 5.1.

Furthermore, the metaweights to derive the holistic acceptability indices are obtained as

$$\alpha^{14} = (1.00, 0.69, 0.54, 0.44, 0.36, 0.30, 0.25, 0.20, 0.16, 0.13, 0.10, 0.07, 0.05, 0.02)$$

Table 5.1 Interval supplier selection matrix

Supplier	Criteria				
	finance	quality	service	flexibility	partnership	risk
1	[0.0457,0.0600]	[0.0457,0.0600]	[0.0370,0.0485]	[0.0370,0.0457]	[0.0400,0.0500]	[0.0385,0.0457]
2	[0.0385,0.0400]	[0.0390,0.0400]	[0.0370,0.0390]	[0.0370,0.0390]	[0.0390,0.0400]	[0.0385,0.0400]
3	[0.0914,0.1200]	[0.0914,0.1200]	[0.0741,0.0970]	[0.0741.0.0914]	[0.0800,0.1000]	[0.0770,0.0914]
4	[0.0600,0.0714]	[0.0600,0.0714]	[0.0670,0.0741]	[0.0714,0.0770]	[0.0700,0.0800]	[0.0714,0.0800]
5	[0.0400,0.0570]	[0.0400,0.0514]	[0.0514,0.0741]	[0.0514,0.0741]	[0.0400,0.0514]	[0.0400,0.0570]
6	[0.0970,0.1200]	[0.1047,0.1200]	[0.0741,0.1047]	[0.0741,0.1047]	[0.1047,0.1200]	[0.0970,0.1200]
7	[0.0904,0.1200]	[0.0800,0.1200]	[0.0904,0.1156]	[0.0756,0.1111]	[0.0400,0.0904]	[0.0400,0.0904]
8	[0.0785,0.1200]	[0.0923,0.1200]	[0.0370,0.0923]	[0.0370,0.0923]	[0.0923,0.1200]	[0.0785,0.1200]
9	[0.0580,0.0670]	[0.0500,0.0600]	[0.0580,0.0741]	[0.0570,0.0741]	[0.0400,0.0580]	[0.0400,0.0580]
10	[0.0600,0.0847]	[0.0600,0.0900]	[0.0637,0.0847]	[0.0741,0.0970]	[0.0847,0.1200]	[0.0847,0.1200]
11	[0.0400,0.0756]	[0.0400,0.0637]	[0.0637,0.1111]	[0.0637,0.1111]	[0.0400,0.0637]	[0.0400,0.0756]
12	[0.0400,0.0647]	[0.0400,0.0647]	[0.0570,0.0741]	[0.0647,0.0770]	[0.0600,0.0800]	[0.0647,0.0800]
13	[0.0600,0.0856]	[0.0500,0.0704]	[0.0704,0.1111]	[0.0704,0.1111]	[0.0400,0.0704]	[0.0400,0.0756]
14	[0.0485,0.0723]	[0.0600,0.0900]	[0.0370,0.0723]	[0.0370,0.0785]	[0.0723,0.1200]	[0.0723,0.1200]

The implementation of SMAA-2 method could be easily realized in terms of an open source programming presented by Tervonen (2014).

5.4.1 Normal distribution

This work assumes that the uncertain and interval-valued data $\left[\underline{a}_{ij}, \bar{a}_{ij}\right]$ follow normal distribution, the average and variance of which are represented as $\mu_i^j = \dfrac{\underline{a}_{ij} + \bar{a}_{ij}}{2}$ and $\left(\sigma^2\right)_i^j = \dfrac{\bar{a}_{ij} - \underline{a}_{ij}}{6}$, respectively. The results about the rank acceptability indices and the holistic acceptability indices derived according to SMAA-2 are demonstrated in Table 5.2 and graphically reported in Figure 5.1.

Based upon the holistic acceptability indices in Table 5.2, we obtain a full and comprehensive rank of all suppliers:

$$6 \succ 3 \succ 7 \succ 8 \succ 10 \succ 13 \succ 14 \succ 4 \succ 11 \succ 12 \succ 9 \succ 2 \succ 5 \succ 1.$$

The selected suppliers are suppliers 6, 3, 7, 8 and 10. More specifically, the most favorable supplier is supplier 6, the holistic rank index of which is 97.08 percent and the first ranking position support is 91 percent, while the least favorable supplier is supplier 1, the holistic rank index and the last rank support of which are 3.07 percent and 64 percent of the possibility, respectively.

5.4.2 Uniform distribution

This study alternatively assumes that the interval-valued data alternatively follow uniform distribution. With such assumptions, this work reports the holistic acceptability indices and the rank acceptability indices in Table 5.3 and Figure 5.2.

It is observed that the sequence of candidate suppliers using SMAA-2 under uniform distribution are: $6 \succ 3 \succ 7 \succ 8 \succ 10 \succ 13 \succ 14 \succ 4 \succ 11 \succ 12 \succ 9 \succ 5 \succ 2 \succ 1$, and the selected suppliers are suppliers 6, 3, 7, 8 and 10 as well. This sequence is mildly different from that derived from norm distribution case. The only difference lies in the rank positions of suppliers 2 and 5. In details, the most favorable supplier 6's holistic rank index is 93.59 percent and first ranking position support is 82 percent, both of which are lower than that of normal distribution case. Meanwhile, the holistic rank index and last rank support possibility of the least favorable supplier 1 are 3.62 percent and 41 percent, respectively.

In summary, SMAA-2 under both the normal distribution and uniform distribution assumptions may produce complete ranks with sufficient discrimination power among all alternatives, in the case that each expert has uncertain evaluations across all suppliers.

Table 5.2 Holistic acceptability indices and rank acceptability indices (normal distribution)

Supplier	b^1	b^2	b^3	b^4	b^5	b^6	b^7	b^8	b^9	b^{10}	b^{11}	b^{12}	b^{13}	b^{14}	a^b
1	0.00	0.00	0.00	0.00	0.00	0.00	0.00	0.00	0.00	0.00	0.00	0.01	0.35	0.64	0.0307
2	0.01	0.01	0.00	0.01	0.02	0.03	0.03	0.02	0.04	0.04	0.08	0.11	0.27	0.33	0.0960
3	0.00	0.25	0.46	0.23	0.05	0.00	0.00	0.00	0.00	0.00	0.00	0.00	0.00	0.00	0.5392
4	0.00	0.00	0.00	0.00	0.00	0.09	0.47	0.38	0.07	0.00	0.00	0.00	0.00	0.00	0.2311
5	0.00	0.00	0.00	0.00	0.00	0.00	0.00	0.00	0.00	0.00	0.04	0.55	0.37	0.03	0.0607
6	0.91	0.08	0.01	0.00	0.00	0.00	0.00	0.00	0.00	0.00	0.00	0.00	0.00	0.00	0.9708
7	0.07	0.24	0.16	0.16	0.21	0.12	0.03	0.01	0.00	0.00	0.00	0.00	0.00	0.00	0.5128
8	0.03	0.24	0.18	0.26	0.17	0.06	0.05	0.02	0.01	0.00	0.00	0.00	0.00	0.00	0.5035
9	0.00	0.00	0.00	0.00	0.00	0.00	0.00	0.00	0.03	0.10	0.59	0.27	0.01	0.00	0.0962
10	0.02	0.17	0.17	0.26	0.31	0.09	0.01	0.00	0.00	0.00	0.00	0.00	0.00	0.00	0.4833
11	0.00	0.00	0.00	0.01	0.03	0.08	0.13	0.12	0.22	0.29	0.10	0.01	0.00	0.00	0.1798
12	0.00	0.00	0.00	0.00	0.00	0.00	0.01	0.13	0.31	0.39	0.14	0.03	0.00	0.00	0.1464
13	0.01	0.00	0.01	0.05	0.09	0.28	0.14	0.20	0.16	0.06	0.01	0.00	0.00	0.00	0.2630
14	0.00	0.01	0.01	0.02	0.12	0.25	0.13	0.12	0.16	0.11	0.05	0.03	0.00	0.00	0.2426

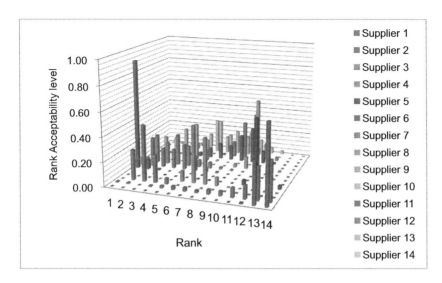

Figure 5.1 Rank acceptability indices (normal distribution)

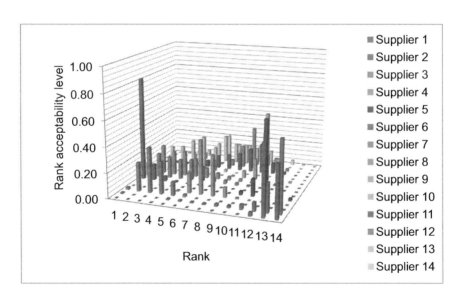

Figure 5.2 Rank acceptability indices (uniform distribution)

Table 5.3 Holistic acceptability indices and rank acceptability indices (uniform distribution)

Supplier	b^1	b^2	b^3	b^4	b^5	b^6	b^7	b^8	b^9	b^{10}	b^{11}	b^{12}	b^{13}	b^{14}	a^b
1	0.00	0.00	0.00	0.00	0.00	0.00	0.00	0.00	0.00	0.00	0.00	0.03	0.55	0.41	0.0362
2	0.01	0.00	0.00	0.00	0.01	0.01	0.01	0.01	0.02	0.02	0.04	0.07	0.23	0.56	0.0587
3	0.02	0.23	0.36	0.26	0.11	0.02	0.00	0.00	0.00	0.00	0.00	0.00	0.00	0.00	0.5321
4	0.00	0.00	0.00	0.00	0.01	0.16	0.43	0.32	0.08	0.01	0.00	0.00	0.00	0.00	0.2365
5	0.00	0.00	0.00	0.00	0.00	0.00	0.00	0.00	0.00	0.03	0.14	0.61	0.20	0.02	0.0708
6	0.82	0.13	0.04	0.01	0.00	0.00	0.00	0.00	0.00	0.00	0.00	0.00	0.00	0.00	0.9359
7	0.10	0.19	0.17	0.16	0.17	0.12	0.04	0.03	0.02	0.01	0.00	0.00	0.00	0.00	0.5103
8	0.03	0.23	0.19	0.20	0.15	0.08	0.05	0.03	0.02	0.01	0.01	0.01	0.00	0.00	0.4813
9	0.00	0.00	0.00	0.00	0.00	0.00	0.00	0.01	0.06	0.17	0.55	0.19	0.01	0.00	0.1025
10	0.02	0.17	0.18	0.24	0.28	0.09	0.02	0.00	0.00	0.00	0.00	0.00	0.00	0.00	0.4717
11	0.00	0.01	0.01	0.02	0.05	0.10	0.12	0.14	0.19	0.24	0.09	0.02	0.00	0.00	0.1995
12	0.00	0.00	0.00	0.00	0.00	0.01	0.05	0.18	0.34	0.31	0.10	0.02	0.00	0.00	0.1592
13	0.01	0.01	0.03	0.05	0.11	0.22	0.16	0.16	0.14	0.10	0.01	0.00	0.00	0.00	0.2687
14	0.00	0.01	0.03	0.05	0.12	0.20	0.13	0.13	0.13	0.10	0.06	0.04	0.01	0.00	0.2495

5.5 Discussion

This chapter is initially engaged in this tremendous surge by first formulating the interval values to optimize and then innovatively applying the SMAA-2 method to obtain an overall rank over all candidate suppliers. The interval data are assumed to be either normally or uniformly distributed in this study, and a metaweight scheme to derive holistic rank indices is elicited from the previous literature. A numerical example using the simulated data is examined to show the effectiveness of SMAA-2.

This paper not only provides the decision maker with more methodological options, but it also enriches the theory and method of the supplier selection problem. Future research should consider the determination of the uncertain sets for decision making and investigate more practical distributions over the uncertainties.

6 Robust supplier selection in the presence of uncertain demand

6.1 Introduction

Outsourcing is typically performed in terms of strategic agreements between a company and some external suppliers, under the regulations of which, the company transfers its internal production functions of goods and services to the external suppliers (Cao and Wang, 2007). The suppliers providing the functions are usually specialists and experts in particular industries. Recently, outsourcing part or all of business processes, ranging from manufacturing to services to logistics and transportation, has progressively emerged as a mainstream in these areas. The outsourcing business model has already leveraged about 40 percent of Fortune 500 corporations including Lucent, GE, Adidas, Microsoft, Oracle and Apple et al. The offshore outsourcing business model can effectively save 50 percent to 70 percent of costs depending on the outsourcing and the onsite resource. Researchers in economics have predicted that by 2015, over US$136 billion worth of wages and 3.3 million US jobs would be outsourced to developing Asian and African countries because of the cheaper labour markets.

Outsourcing strategy could bring out several benefits to different stakeholders, including: (1) decreased cost from economies of scale; (2) market uncertainty transferred to the upstream suppliers; (3) capital investment moved to the upstream suppliers; (4) emphasis on the core competency; (5) free riding of suppliers' new technologies innovation to cut down product development life cycles.

After a buyer makes the decision to perform outsourcing, the most critical step is supplier management, which involves choosing the appropriate suppliers and then allocating tasks to selected suppliers. More specifically, the buyer definitely needs to decide which suppliers to cooperate with and how many tasks to allocate to selected suppliers. The business process of supplier selection and allocation could be recognized as a representation of the rent-seeking game, where many competitors compete for prizes. The possibility that a supplier would be selected is positively related to the supplier's service level and negatively related to the outsourcing cost (Benjaafar et al., 2007). With respect to supplier allocation, the buyer usually considers the requirements in terms of production capacity and upper bound constraints about allocating demand among different suppliers.

This study investigates the problem of supplier selection and allocation in the process of outsourcing under an uncertain environment for the purpose of minimizing the buyer's total expenditure. At the start of each planning period, the buyer predicts the market demand associated with each product. After collecting the market information, the buyer meets and negotiates with candidate suppliers about detailed items of the outsourcing contract, i.e. the Service Level Agreement (SLA) and prices. The final deals are determined on the basis of many iterations of such a negotiation process. The price determined with each selected supplier is unchanged, regardless of any possible market fluctuations. A Service Level Agreement (SLA) is an official requirement embedded in the outsourcing contracts which defines the ranges of the outsourcing task in terms of goods and services that the supplier will provide to its customer, the volume of work that will be accepted and delivered and the quality of goods and services (Fu, Lai and Liang, 2016). In this thesis, the Service Level Agreement (SLA) is denoted by a minimum quantity commitment (MQC) regulated by the buyer, which stipulates a minimum quantity that must be allocated to each selected supplier. As a safeguard against overreliance on a particular supplier, the risk-averse buyer would select a lower limit number of suppliers and set many quantity limits on production arrangements allocated to an individual supplier.

In this chapter, we model the supplier selection and allocation problem in the presence of uncertain demand using a stochastic programming formulation and use a new robust optimization approach to derive the robust solution scheme in an uncertain environment. The obtained results are effectively less sensitive to any realization of uncertainty. The buyer's total expected expenditure in outsourcing process varies with his attitudes towards risk and penalty parameters measuring absolute deviation in demand. Through adjusting penalty parameters, the buyer can effectively decide on an optimal supplier selection and allocation scheme while sufficiently using all suppliers' capacities.

6.2 Problem description

The supplier selection and allocation problem faced by a buyer investigated in this thesis is described as follows. We consider the case that a buyer owns I products to be outsourced to J suppliers. The uncertain market demand for product i is denoted by U_i. The quoted price issued by supplier j to produce per unit of product i is $p_{i,j}$. In the case of the quoted price being accepted by the buyer, each buyer–supplier pair reaches a consensus about the service level. In this study, the minimum quantity commitments (MQC) v_j regulated on the selected suppliers are used to guarantee the realization of a Service Level Agreement (SLA), which describes the minimum quantity that should be allocated to the selected supplier.

In order to diversify risk and assure outsourced tasks are under control, the buyer stipulates that with respect to each product, a minimum number of suppliers N_i should be selected, taking into account the existing capacity of each supplier. This requirement could protect the buyer from the occurrence of a single supplier being inadequate to supply or the delaying delivery. Nevertheless, simply rejecting to put all eggs in one basket is not enough. For example, in the case of a buyer outsourcing his production arrangements to at least five suppliers and the respective assignment condition is 96 percent, 1 percent, 1 percent, 1 percent, 1 percent, it is nearly the same as arranging all tasks to the first supplier. Therefore, the risk-averse buyer will require an upper bound about percentage allocation A_j of production tasks for each supplier j, i.e. the amount of product i to be outsourced to supplier j can then be at most $A_j \cdot U_i$. Sadrian and Yoon (1994) and Lim et al. (2011) have previously incorporated such quantity limits in their research papers as well.

Notations for decision variables and parameters used in this study are presented as:

1 $x_{i,j}$: a nonnegative decision variable representing the quantity of product i outsourced to supplier j.
2 $y_{i,j}$: a binary decision variable equal to 1 if supplier j is selected to manufacture product i and 0 otherwise.
3 $p_{i,j}$: a parameter denoting the quoted price issued by supplier j to manufacture per unit of product i.
4 v_j: a parameter representing the minimum total quantity of all products that should be allocated to supplier j.
5 A_j: the maximum allocation for supplier j.
6 U_i: the uncertain market demand of product i.
7 $A_j U_i$: the maximum quantity of product i that could be arranged to supplier j.
8 N_i: the minimum number of suppliers to be selected to manufacture product i.
9 M: a sufficiently large positive number.

The following constraints (6.1) guarantee that any selected supplier j has to be allocated at least v_j production tasks, thus assuring the commitment of the service level of the selected supplier:

$$v_j \sum_{i=1}^{I} y_{i,j} \leq \sum_{i=1}^{I} x_{i,j} \leq M \sum_{i=1}^{I} y_{i,j}, \, j = 1, 2, \ldots, J. \tag{6.1}$$

Constraints (6.2) below give quantity regulations on each supplier for diversifying the buyer's risk:

$$x_{i,j} \leq A_j U_i y_{i,j}, \, i = 1, 2, \ldots, I, \, j = 1, 2, \ldots, J. \tag{6.2}$$

The following constraints (6.3) denote that the buyer makes its decision based upon the forecasted demand:

$$\sum_{j=1}^{J} x_{i,j} \leq U_i. \tag{6.3}$$

Constraints (6.4) below represent that for product i, the number of selected suppliers must be no less than the specified number of suppliers N_i:

$$\sum_{j=1}^{J} y_{i,j} \geq N_i. \tag{6.4}$$

Consequently, for the purpose of minimizing the buyer's total expected expenditure in the process of outsourcing, we present the basic mathematical model (6.5) as below:

$$\text{Min} \sum_{i=1}^{I}\sum_{j=1}^{J} p_{i,j} x_{i,j}$$

$$\text{s.t.} \quad v_j \sum_{i=1}^{I} y_{i,j} \leq \sum_{i=1}^{I} x_{i,j} \leq M \sum_{i=1}^{I} y_{i,j}, \forall j$$

$$x_{i,j} \leq A_j U_i y_{i,j}, \forall i, j.$$

$$\sum_{j=1}^{J} x_{i,j} \leq U_i, \forall i. \tag{6.5}$$

$$\sum_{j=1}^{J} y_{i,j} \geq N_i, \forall i$$

$$y_{i,j} \in \{0,1\}.$$

$$x_{i,j} \geq 0.$$

for all $i = 1, 2, \ldots I, j = 1, 2, \ldots J$.

6.3 Stochastic formulation and robust optimization solution scheme

The developed basic mathematical model (6.5) is a linear integer programming formulation. However, parameters U_i in (6.5) are always unknown at the start of the planning period. Conventional wisdom may expect to handle this issue through replacing these parameters by the corresponding best point estimators. For example, it is natural and reasonable to use the expected value $E(U_i)$ to replace the aforementioned uncertain parameters U_i. Nevertheless, one significant drawback of this approach is the obtained solutions cannot be always guaranteed as feasible. Sometimes, decision makers may perform effective sensitivity analysis to improve the quality of the relative solutions. This approach to find optimal solutions is typically regarded as a reactive approach. Lai and Ng (2005) argued that in practice decision makers usually prefer employing proactive schemes to derive their solutions. A typical proactive approach in literature is robust optimization, which integrates the goal programming and the scenario-based description of uncertainty set (Mulvey et al., 1995). When it is impossible to eliminate the uncertainty completely, the best choice for decision makers is to accept the uncertainty first, and then understand and incorporate it into the decision-making process.

The problems in the presence of uncertainty solved by robust optimization approach involve a set of scenarios $\Omega = \{1, 2, \ldots, S\}$. With respect to each scenario, the respective probability is represented by φs such that $\sum_{s=1}^{S} \varphi_s = 1$. The philosophy of robust optimization is proceeding around the trade-off between solution robustness and model robustness, which are respectively presented as follows:

> **Definition 6.1** (Solution robustness). An optimal solution is solution robust with respect to optimality if it remains 'close' to optimal for any realization of the scenario $s \in \Omega$.
>
> **Definition 6.2** (Model robustness). An optimal solution is model robust with respect to feasibility if it remains 'almost' feasible for any realization of the scenario $s \in \Omega$.

Finally, a robust optimization formulation of the basic mathematical model (6.5) is given as below:

$$
\text{Min} \quad
\begin{aligned}
&\sum_{s=1}^{S}\varphi_s\sum_{i=1}^{I}\sum_{j=1}^{J}p_{i,j}^{s}x_{i,j} + \lambda\sum_{s=1}^{S}\varphi_s\left|\sum_{i=1}^{I}\sum_{j=1}^{J}p_{i,j}^{s}x_{i,j} - \sum_{s=1}^{S}\varphi_s\sum_{i=1}^{I}\sum_{j=1}^{J}p_{i,j}^{s}x_{i,j}\right| \\
&\sum_{s=1}^{S}\varphi_s\sum_{i=1}^{I}w_i\left|U_i^{s} - \sum_{j=1}^{J}x_{i,j}\right|
\end{aligned}
$$

$$
\text{s.t.} \quad v_j\sum_{i=1}^{I}y_{i,j} \leq \sum_{i=1}^{I}x_{i,j} \leq M\sum_{i=1}^{I}y_{i,j}, \forall j
$$

$$
x_{i,j} \leq \min_{s \in \Omega}\left\{A_j U_i^{s} y_{i,j}\right\}, \forall i, j
$$

$$
\sum_{j=1}^{J}x_{i,j} \leq \max_{s \in \Omega}\left\{U_i^{s}\right\}, \forall i. \tag{6.6}
$$

$$
\sum_{j=1}^{J}y_{i,j} \geq N_i, \forall i.
$$

$$
y_{i,j} \in \{0,1\}.
$$

$$
x_{i,j} \geq 0.
$$

for all $i = 1, 2, \ldots I, j = 1, 2, \ldots J.$

where λ and w_i are non-negative parameters.

The first term of the objective function in (6.6) is the buyer's expected expenditure in outsourcing, and the second term is the mean absolute deviation (MAD) of the expected expenditure. The fluctuations of expenditure among different scenarios inevitably cause a larger value of the mean absolute deviation. Then the penalty would be increased. Parameter λ performs as a risk trade-off factor between expected expenditure and deviation here. According to the above two definitions, the first and second terms in the objective functions can be regarded as a measurement of solution robustness, and the absolute deviations in the third term of the objective function are viewed as the evaluations of model robustness. Because of that, parameters w_i are non-negative penalty weightings; when the constraints are violated (i.e. solutions are not sufficiently model robust), a larger penalty would be assigned to the objective function. Through employing the mean absolute values as penalties and using constraints $\sum_{j=1}^{J} x_{i,j} \leq \max_{s \in \Omega}\{U_i^s\}, \forall i$, the model can generate solutions that are immune to the descriptions of various scenarios (Lai and Ng, 2005).

Because of the occurrence of the absolute values in the objective function, the model cannot be directly solved using commonly available linear optimization software. Traditionally, absolute deviations have been replaced by incorporating positive and negative deviation variables. In recent years, a simple and efficient linearization approach to transforming the absolute deviation into linear terms was developed by Yu and Li (2000), which solely requires introducing one new variable. We employ this novel transformation due to the ease of computation. The proposed linearization method transforming the absolute deviation into linear formulations is introduced as below.

Theorem 6.1 (Yu and Li, (2000)). A goal programming:

$$\text{Minimize } Z = |f(x) - g| \tag{6.7}$$
$$\text{Subject to } x \, \varepsilon \, F.$$

F is a feasible set and (6.7) can be linearized using the following transformation:

$$\text{Minimize } Z' = f(x) - g + 2\delta \tag{6.8}$$
$$\text{Subject to } f(x) - g + \delta \geq 0, \, \delta \geq 0, \, x \, \varepsilon \, F.$$

Proof. Because the newly introduced variable δ in the objective function of (6.8) has a positive coefficient, for the purpose of minimizing Z' in (6.8), δ should guarantee its minimum value. Considering the associated constraints in (6.8), we have $\delta \geq g - f(x)$ and $\delta \geq 0$. In other words, the minimum value of δ is $\max\{g - f(x), 0\}$.

If $g - f(x) \leq 0$, we obtain $\delta = 0$. Hence, $Z' = f(x) - g = Z$. However, on the other hand, if $g - f(x) > 0$, we have $\delta = g - f(x)$. Finally, $Z' = g - f(x) = Z$. Consequently, the two formulations (6.7) and (6.8) are equivalent. The proof of **Theorem 6.1** is then completed.

For the purpose of applying **Theorem 6.1** to the model (6.6), two non-negative variables z^s and h_i^s for scenarios are randomly generated, where $s \, \varepsilon \, \Omega$.

Therefore, model (6.6) could be transformed into the following formulation, where λ and w_i are weighting parameters:

$$
\begin{aligned}
\text{Min } & \sum_{s=1}^{S}\varphi_s\sum_{i=1}^{I}\sum_{j=1}^{J}p_{i,j}^s + \lambda\sum_{s=1}^{S}\varphi_s\left(\sum_{i=1}^{I}\sum_{j=1}^{j}p_{i,j}^s x_{i,j} - \sum_{s=1}^{S}\varphi_s\sum_{i=1}^{I}\sum_{j=1}^{J}p_{i,j}^s x_{i,j} + 2z^s\right)\\
& + \sum_{s=1}^{S}\varphi_s\sum_{i=1}^{I}w_i\left(U_i^s - \sum_{j=1}^{J}x_{i,j} + 2b_i^s\right)
\end{aligned}
$$

s.t. $\quad v_j\sum_{i=1}^{I}y_{i,j} \leq \sum_{i=1}^{I}x_{i,j} \leq M\sum_{i=1}^{I}y_{i,j}, \forall j$

$x_{i,j} \leq \min_{s\in\Omega}\left\{A_j U_i^s y_{i,j}\right\}, \forall i, j$

$\sum_{j=1}^{J}x_{i,j} \leq \max_{s\in\Omega}\left\{U_i^s\right\}, \forall i.$ $\qquad(6.9)$

$\sum_{i=1}^{I}\sum_{j=1}^{j}p_{i,j}^s x_{i,j} - \sum_{s=1}^{S}\varphi_s\sum_{i=1}^{I}\sum_{j=1}^{J}p_{i,j}^s x_{i,j} + z^s \geq 0.$

$U_i^s - \sum_{j=1}^{J}x_{i,j} + b_i^s \geq 0.$

$\sum_{j=1}^{J}y_{i,j} \geq N_i, \forall i.$

$y_{i,j} \in \{0,1\}.$

$x_{i,j}, b_i^s, z^s \geq 0.$

for all $i = 1, 2, \ldots I, j = 1, 2, \ldots J.$

The mathematical model (6.9) is now a standard integer programming that can be easily solved using a commercial software package such as Ceplex, Matlab and LINDO (Shrage, 1997).

6.4   Numerical illustrations and managerial implications

6.4.1   Numerical illustrations

This section investigates the case in which the buyer is planning to take different future demand scenarios associated with different products into account in its strategic planning, while the candidate suppliers release their quoted prices in each scenario. For ease of demonstration, we assume a buyer would like to outsource two products ($I = 2$) to five candidate suppliers ($J = 5$), and the required minimum number of selected suppliers for products 1 and 2 are three and four, respectively. Market demand and quoted prices are heavily dependent upon economic conditions. We assume that possible future economic conditions are boom, good, fair and poor, and the corresponding probabilities are 0.40, 0.25, 0.20 and 0.15 (Dupacova et al., 2000). Data related to the presented supplier selection and allocation problem are shown in Tables 6.1 to 6.3.

The risk trade-off factor λ and all weighting parameters w_i are set to be 1. The optimal solutions are then obtained and summarized in Table 6.4.

Table 6.1 Prices quoted by suppliers

Product	Economic Situation	Supplier				
		1	2	3	4	5
1	Boom	7	8	7	8	7
	Fair	5	7	5	6	6
	Good	4	5	4	5	5
	Poor	2	3	3	4	3
2	Boom	8	9	8	9	8
	Fair	6	8	6	7	7
	Good	5	6	5	6	6
	Poor	3	4	4	5	4

Table 6.2 Projected market demand under each economic situation

Product	Economic situation			
	Boom	Fair	Good	Poor
1	120	100	85	70
2	150	95	90	75
Probability	0.40	0.25	0.20	0.15

Table 6.3 The minimum quantity commitment (v_j) and upper bound allocation (A_j) for each supplier

	Supplier				
	1	2	3	4	5
v_j	30	32	25	24	28
A_j	50%	50%	50%	50%	55%

Table 6.4 Optimal solutions

	Supplier				
	1	2	3	4	5
Product 1	0	0	35	35	35
Product 2	30	0	15	13	21
Expected expenditure			1388.48		

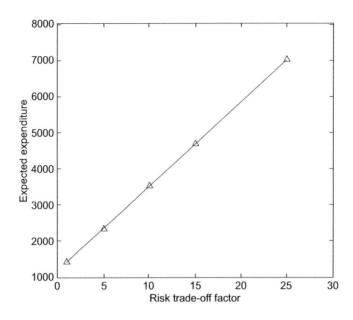

Figure 6.1 The relationship between expected expenditure and risk trade-off factor

6.4.2 Risk trade-off factors

Previous literature (Lai and Ng, 2005) suggest that different values of the risk trade-off factor λ denote the decision maker's degree of risk aversion. Figure 6.1 reports the relationship between expected expenditure and risk trade-off factor. It is noticed that in general, the expected expenditure is positively proportional to the risk trade-off factor λ. In cases where the risk trade-off factor λ is sufficiently large, the expected expenditure nearly approaches positive infinity.

That is, if a decision maker is very conservative towards risk, the final decision is not to open the business.

6.4.3 Trade-off between solution robustness and model robustness

The process of proving Theorem 6.1 indicates the possibility of solution infeasibility, i.e. when $\sum_{j}^{J} x_{i,j} > U_i^s$, $h_i^s = \sum_{j}^{J} x_{i,j} - U_i^s > 0$. An infeasible solution is obtained when $h_i^s > 0$. The robust optimization approach accepts minor infeasibility in the constraints by means of penalty parameters w_i, which find the trade-off between solution robustness and model robustness in this thesis (Mulvey et al., 1995). Therefore, it is necessary to verify the developed robust optimization with fluctuant penalty parameters w_i, as demonstrated in Figure 6.2.

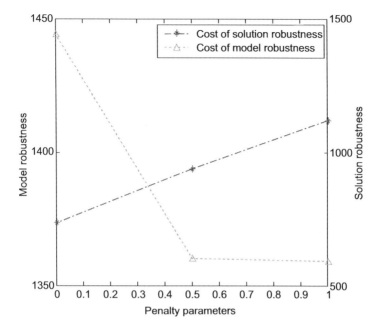

Figure 6.2 Trade-off between solution robustness and model robustness

As depicted in Figure 6.2, in the case of penalty parameters w_i increase, the obtained solution approaches to be almost feasible at the price of solution robustness. Furthermore, there exists a sole penalty parameter w_i, at which point decision makers can derive a robust solution through a trade-off between solution robustness (optimality) and model robustness (feasibility).

6.5 Discussion

This section develops a stochastic programming model to solve the supplier selection and allocation problem in outsourcing in an environment with uncertainty. A new robust optimization approach is deployed to find solutions to this problem under different economic conditions, which is capable of providing credible and reliable solutions to many practical problems. A decision maker's attitude towards risk and the penalty parameters for demand deviation are introduced into the objective function. A simple and efficient linearization method is then applied to convert the absolute value in objective function into a linear expression. Numerical illustrations are provided with managerial implications to support strategic decision making. The trade-off between optimality and feasibility supports decision makers in finding robust solutions.

The developed robust optimization mechanism in this study can be directly applied to other optimization problems arisen in real life, i.e. hotel revenue management (Lai and Ng, 2005), professional services firms revenue optimization (Lai et al., 2007) and aggregate production planning (Leung and Wu, 2004). Future research should take into consideration other aspects like minimum allocation under different economic situations, operational decisions for each supplier based on different production capacity requirements and competition among different suppliers.

7 Production capacity planning via robust optimization

7.1 Introduction

Production capacity planning is the process of determining how much production capacity to acquire and how to plan its utilization to meet fluctuant market demands (Escudero et al., 1993), which is typically arisen in manufacturing industry. This uncertainty generally leads to uneven or unpredictable capacity utilization. In the context of capacity planning – capacity is considered as the maximum amount of techniques, raw materials, skilled manpower, machines and other production facilities – all of these factors can be integrated to be the amount of plants. The traditional way of dealing with uncertain demand is to collect opinions from a group of experienced managers and then select the most likely forecast of demand for different products. The capacity is planned such that all plants have a sufficiently high utilization while fulfilling the projected demand. However, such capacity planning has often resulted in either lower utilization of capacity if the actual demand materialized is less than the projected, or additional cost associated with capacity expansion if the actual demand is higher (Swaminathan, 2000). Managers in the manufacturing industry are significantly interested in developing an effective capacity planning policy that enables hedging against the uncertainty.

Capacity planning typically consists of two parts: (1) plant building decisions have to be made before the actual market demand is realized and (2) once the demand is materialized, different types of orders representing different demands need to be allocated to different plants, with the objective to minimize the weighted sum of the total investment required for building the plants and the additional cost associated with capacity expansion. Although plant building decisions have to be made long before the actual market demand is realized, business management needs to incorporate knowledge on how to utilize the plants when the actual demand is materialized while making plant building plans (Swaminathan, 2000). Furthermore, in the decision-making process, managers are obliged to face a trade-off between fixed costs and additional costs associated with capacity expansion when market demand fluctuates (Paraskevopoulos et al., 1991). This involves maintenance of existing capacity and capacity expansion in response to excessive demand. In this chapter, we address the plant building decision and assignment of orders to plants in the presence of uncertain status of capacity utilization and propose methods to operationally hedge against the uncertainty.

The uncertainty inherent in forecasting unanticipated status of capacity utilization makes it unrealistic and unreliable to make the aforementioned decisions only on the strength of deterministic models. In general, a nominal 'optimal' solution derived from one particular prediction of unknown parameters may often no longer be feasible or even optimal, if this forecast is not realized (Aghezzaf, 2005). Furthermore, Mula et al. (2006) argued that models for production planning without recognizing the uncertainty would lead to inferior capacity planning decisions when compared to models that explicitly incorporate the uncertainty. When it is impossible to eliminate the uncertainty completely, the best choice for decision makers is to recognize and accept the uncertainty first, and then understand and incorporate it into the decision-making process. Therefore, it is natural to develop models that are immune to data uncertainty, which are described as 'robust'. Robust optimization is an approach that ensures the solutions remain feasible and near optimal when data change (Soyster, 1973; Ben-Tal and Nemirovski, 2000, 2002; Bertsimas and Sim, 2004; Denton et al., 2010). Two practically appealing advantages of robust optimization make this methodology gain substantial popularity for solving some types of stochastic optimization problems: (1) the robust counterpart remains computationally tractable and independent of the number of uncertain parameters and (2) the precise information of the distribution but mild assumptions on bounded support of the uncertain data is not required (José Alem and Morabito, 2012).

The purpose of this chapter is three-fold. First, we propose a computationally tractable robust optimization model to solve the capacity planning problem in the presence of uncertainty, with minimization of total investment in building plants and the additional cost associated with capacity expansion. Our robust optimization framework extends previous work of Denton et al. (2010) to the capacity planning problem and develops robust schemes for manufacturing managers while facing the uncertain status of capacity utilization to fulfill fluctuant orders. Second, we seek to construct a robust order-to-plant assignment scheme that trades off two competing criteria: (1) the fixed cost of building individual plants and (2) the total cost associated with capacity expansion across all plants. Third, we test the effectiveness of the proposed model by making comparisons between the solutions derived from a deterministic model with nominal values and the proposed modified robust version of capacity planning model (MR-CP).

7.2   Deterministic production capacity planning problem

In order to fulfill the forecast demand, manufacturing managers have to make plant building plans before the actual demand is known, with the risk of capacity shortage and oversupply, and after the realization of demand, decide on possible capacity expansion and order-to-plant assignment schemes. Although plant building decisions have to be made long before the actual demand is realized, management needs to incorporate information on how to utilize the plants when the actual demand is materialized while making plant building decisions. The objective is to minimize the total fixed cost of plant building and the additional cost associated with capacity expansion, with sufficient utilization of capacity to meet market demand.

Indices

1 i: index for blocks of orders, $i = 1, 2, \ldots, m$.
2 j: index for plants, $j = 1, 2, \ldots n$.

Parameters

1 λ_{ij}: actual capacity utilization to fulfill order i in plant j, $\lambda_{ij} \in [\underline{\lambda}_i, \overline{\lambda}_i]$ $\underline{\lambda}_i$ and $\overline{\lambda}_i$ are lower and upper bounds on the utilization status of capacity to fulfill order i, respectively, $i = 1, 2, \ldots, m$, $j = 1, 2, \ldots, n$.
2 M_i: minimum number of plants to be selected to fulfill order i, $i = 1, 2, \ldots, m$.
3 N_j: maximum number of orders that can be allocated to plant j, $j = 1, 2, \ldots, n$.
4 R_j: regular capacity of plant j, $j = 1, 2, \ldots, n$.
5 c_j^f: fixed cost to build plant j, $j = 1, 2, \ldots, n$.
6 c_j^v: variable cost per unit of expanded capacity in plant j, $j = 1, 2, \ldots, n$.

Decision variables

1 x_j: a binary decision variable equal to 1 if plant j is built and 0 otherwise.
2 y_{ij}: a binary decision variable equal to 1 if order i is allocated to plant j and 0 otherwise.
3 e_j: level of capacity expansion in plant j.

The deterministic capacity planning model (D-CP) is developed as a bench-mark when the capacity utilization status is known with certainty. Recall that the objective of the capacity planning problem is to minimize the weighted sum of the total investment in building plants and the additional cost associated with capacity expansion, which needs to find a trade-off between two competing criteria: (1) the fixed cost of opening individual plants and (2) the additional cost associated with production capacity expansion across all plants.

The deterministic formulation we describe in this section is to decide on the number of plants to build and allocations of orders to plants. Consider the following LP model (D-CP):

$$\min \sum_{j=1}^{n} (c_j^f x_j + c_j^v e_j)$$

s.t.

$$y_{ij} \le x_j, \forall i, j \tag{7.1}$$

$$\sum_{i=1}^{m} y_{ij} \le N_j, \forall j \tag{7.2}$$

$$\sum_{j=1}^{n} y_{ij} \ge M_i, \forall i \tag{7.3}$$

$$\sum_{i=1}^{m} \lambda_{ij} y_{ij} \le R_j x_j + e_j, \forall j \tag{7.4}$$

$$x_j, y_{ij} \in \{0,1\}, e_j \ge 0, \forall i, j. \tag{7.5}$$

Constraints (7.1) indicate the fact that the built plant is not necessarily assigned by orders, which reveals the occurrence of excess capacity. Constraints (7.2) provide an upper limit on the amount of orders to be allocated to a single plant, which prevents order fulfillment from overreliance on a single plant. Constraints (7.3) imply that in order to diversify risk and assure that production is under control, the number of selected plants to fulfill each order must be no less than a specified threshold. Constraints (7.4) assure that total capacity utilization is under control.

Due to the fact that capacity expansion occurs when regular capacity cannot fulfill the allocated orders, it is reasonable to make the following assumption:

$$c_j^v > \min_j \left\{ \frac{c_j^f}{R_j} \right\}, \forall j. \tag{7.6}$$

This assumption stipulates that the cost per unit capacity is greater for expanded capacity than for regular capacity. If assumption (7.6) does not hold, then rational manufacturing managers will open a single plant and allocate all orders to a single plant.

7.3   Robust optimization framework

Note that the proposed deterministic capacity planning model (D-CP) does not always hold in practice. A common problem that is confronted by many manufacturing managers is insufficient information about the actual capacity utilization status at the beginning of a planning period. Therefore, in real life, the proposed deterministic capacity planning model (D-CP) just looks like a mixed integer linear program (MILP). Parameters λ_{ij} in D-CP are always unknown at the beginning of a planning horizon. Decision makers may expect to handle this issue by taking the place of these parameters by the best point estimators. For example, it is extremely common to use the expected value $E(\lambda_{ij})$ to replace the unknown parameters λ_{ij}. However, the significant drawback of this idea is that the obtained solutions cannot be always guaranteed as feasible. Decision makers may conduct sensitivity analysis to improve the quality of solutions. This piece of approach to find optimal solutions is viewed as a reactive approach. Lai and Ng (2005) argued that in practice decision makers prefer using proactive techniques to derive their solutions. A widely used proactive approach in literature is robust optimization. When the decision makers are risk averse, the deployment of robust optimization is appropriate (Wu, 2011).

Recently, robust optimization methodology has emerged as a preeminent tool in immunizing uncertain mathematical optimization. This chapter employs the robust optimization approach to modeling uncertain capacity utilization status as a polyhedral uncertainty set in capacity planning. We mildly assume that decision makers are able to provide appropriate estimations of lower and upper bounds on capacity utilization status to fulfill each order, according to the estimation derived from historical data. The actual capacity utilization, without exact knowledge of distribution, must lie within the aforementioned polyhedral uncertainty set. Our work seeks to minimize the possible worst cost for all realization of capacity utilization of the uncertainty set.

Recall that λ_{ij} indicate actual capacity utilization required to fulfill order i in plant j, $\lambda_{ij} \in [\underline{\lambda}_i, \overline{\lambda}_i]$, $\underline{\lambda}_i$ and $\overline{\lambda}_i$ are lower and upper bounds on the utilization status of capacity to fulfill order i, respectively, $i = 1, 2, \ldots, m$, $j = 1, 2, \ldots, n$. Let:

$$U = \{\lambda_{ij} \mid \lambda_{ij} \in [\underline{\lambda}_i, \overline{\lambda}_i], \sum_{(i,j):y_{ij}=1} \frac{\lambda_{ij} - \underline{\lambda}_i}{\overline{\lambda}_i - \underline{\lambda}_i} \leq \Gamma\}. \quad (7.7)$$

This denotation (7.7) is consistent with the idea of Bertsimas and Sim (2004) and Denton et al. (2010). As a controlled variable, Γ determines the conservative degree of the worst-case scenario is. More specifically, Γ denotes an upper bound on the number of capacity utilization reaching the corresponding worst-case. Thus, in particular, if $\Gamma = 0$, we consider only the best scenario, where all actual capacity utilization takes their lowest values; if $\Gamma = n$, the worst-case scenario is taken into account. Within the framework of capacity planning problem in this chapter, we intuitively take Γ as an integer.

Therefore, the robust version of capacity planning problem (R-CP) is formulated as a two-stage recourse problem below:

$$\min_{(x,y)} \{\sum_{j=1}^{n} c_j^f x_j + \psi(x,y)\}$$

s.t.

$$y_{ij} \leq x_j, \forall i, j$$

$$\sum_{i=1}^{m} y_{ij} \leq N_j, \forall j$$

$$\sum_{j=1}^{n} y_{ij} \geq M_i, \forall i$$

$$x_j, y_{ij} \in (0,1), \forall i, j$$

where

$$\psi(x,y) = \max_{\lambda} \sum_{j=1}^{n} \mu_j$$

s.t.

$$\mu_j = c_j^v \max\{0,(\sum_{i:y_{ij}=1} \lambda_{ij} y_{ij} - R_j x_j)\}, \forall j$$

$$\sum_{(i,j):y_{ij}=1} \frac{\lambda_{ij} - \underline{\lambda}_i}{\overline{\lambda}_i - \underline{\lambda}_i} \leq \Gamma$$

$$\underline{\lambda}_i \leq \lambda_{ij} \leq \overline{\lambda}_i, \forall (i,j): y_{ij} = 1. \tag{7.8}$$

The objective function $\Psi(x,y)$ is to minimize the additional cost with respect to capacity expansion, wherein x and y are unchangeable, and λ_{ij} are decision variables. Note that μ_j equals to either 0 or the difference between the actual capacity utilization and the regular capacity in plant j. Hence, the expression of $\Psi(x,y)$ in (7.8) can be reformulated as follows:

$$\max_{(\lambda,z)} \sum_{j=1}^{n} \{c_j^v (\sum_{i=1}^{m} \lambda_{ij} - R_j x_j) z_j\}$$

s.t.

$$\sum_{i=1}^{m} \sum_{j=1}^{n} \frac{\lambda_{ij} - \underline{\lambda}_i y_{ij} z_j}{\overline{\lambda}_i - \underline{\lambda}_i} \leq \Gamma \tag{7.9}$$

$$\underline{\lambda}_i y_{ij} z_j \leq \lambda_{ij} \leq \overline{\lambda}_i y_{ij} z_j, \forall i, j \tag{7.10}$$

$$z_j \in (0,1), \forall j, \tag{7.11}$$

where

$$z_j = \begin{cases} 0, & \sum_{i=1}^{n} \lambda_{ij} - R_j x_j \leq 0, \\ 1, & \sum_{i=1}^{n} \lambda_{ij} - R_j x_j > 0. \end{cases} \tag{7.12}$$

Since the variables z_j indicate a binary choice, the above reformulation is a nonlinear program. However, the special structure of this reformulation motivates us to transform it into a linear program. Note that constraints (7.10) promise that if $z_j = 0$ for some j, then $\lambda_{ij} = 0$ for all i. This suggests to us to reformulate $\Psi(x,y)$ as a mixed integer linear program (MILP) in the following:

$$\max_{(\lambda,z)}\{\sum_{j=1}^{m}\sum_{i=1}^{n}c_j^v\lambda_{ij} - \sum_{j=1}^{n}(c_j^vR_jx_j)z_j\} \tag{7.13}$$

s.t.

(7.9), (7.10) and (7.11).

For the sake of obtaining the dual of $\Psi(x,y)$, we define $\Omega_{ij} = \dfrac{\lambda_{ij} - \underline{\lambda}_i y_{ij}z_j}{\overline{\lambda}_i - \underline{\lambda}_i}, 0 \leq \Omega_{ij} \leq 1$. Note that constraints (7.10) imply that if λij reaches its lower bound $\underline{\lambda}_i$, Ωij will be 0; if λij is at its upper bound $\overline{\lambda}$, Ωij will be 1. On the basis of this definition, the above reformulated mixed integer linear program (MILP) (7.13) can be expressed as follows:

$$\max_{(\Omega,z)}\{\sum_{i=1}^{m}\sum_{j=1}^{n}c_j^v(\overline{\lambda}_i - \underline{\lambda}_i)\Omega_{ij} - \sum_{j=1}^{n}c_j^v(R_jx_j - \sum_{i=1}^{m}\underline{\lambda}_iy_{ij})z_j\} \tag{7.14}$$

s.t.

$$\sum_{i=1}^{m}\sum_{j=1}^{n}\Omega_{ij} \leq \Gamma \tag{7.15}$$

$$\Omega_{ij} - y_{ij}z_j \leq 0, \forall i, j \tag{7.16}$$

$$z_j \leq 1, \forall j \tag{7.17}$$

$$\Omega_{ij} \geq 0, z_j \geq 0, \forall i, j. \tag{7.18}$$

Intuitively, this reformulation is a mixed integer linear program (MILP) and the decision variables are Ω_{ij} and z_j.

Therefore, the dual of the above reformulation of $\Psi(x,y)$ is:

$$\min_{(\alpha,\beta,\gamma)}\{\alpha\Gamma + \sum_{j=1}^{n}\gamma_j\} \tag{7.19}$$

s.t.

$$\alpha + \beta_{ij} \geq c_j^v(\overline{\lambda}_i - \underline{\lambda}_i), \forall i, j \tag{7.20}$$

$$-\sum_{i=1}^{m}\beta_{ij}y_{ij} + \gamma_j \geq -c_j^v(R_jx_j - \sum_{i=1}^{m}\underline{\lambda}_iy_{ij}), \forall j \tag{7.21}$$

$$\alpha \geq 0, \beta_{ij} \geq 0, \gamma_j \geq 0, \forall i, j. \tag{7.22}$$

Note that α is the dual variable associated with constraint (7.15), β_{ij} the dual variables with respect to constraints (7.16) and γ_j are the dual variables with respect to bounds (7.17).

Recall the two-stage recourse problem (7.8) formulated by the robust version of d capacity planning problem (R-CP); we reformulate (7.8) as follows:

$$\min_{(x,y,\alpha,\beta,\gamma)} \{\sum_{j=1}^{n} c_j^f x_j + \alpha\Gamma + \sum_{j=1}^{n}\gamma_j\}$$

s.t.

$$y_{ij} \le x_j, \forall i, j$$

$$\sum_{i=1}^{m} y_{ij} \le N_j, \forall j$$

$$\sum_{j=1}^{n} y_{ij} \ge M_i, \forall i$$

$$\alpha + \beta_{ij} \ge c_j^v(\overline{\lambda}_i - \underline{\lambda}_i), \forall i, j \tag{7.23}$$

$$-\sum_{i=1}^{m}\beta_{ij}y_{ij} + \gamma_j \ge -c_j^v(R_j x_j - \sum_{i=1}^{m}\underline{\lambda}_i y_{ij}), \forall j \tag{7.24}$$

$$x_j, y_{ij} \in \{0,1\}, \forall i, j$$
$$\alpha \ge 0, \beta_{ij} \ge 0, \gamma_j \ge 0, \forall i, j.$$

The above reformulation is a mixed integer nonlinear program (MINP), due to the multiplication of β_{ij} and y_{ij} in constraints (7.24). Denton et al. (2010) proposed an efficient analysis to deal with this issue, i.e., if $y_{ij} = 0$, then we can set $\beta_{ij} = c_j^v(\overline{\lambda}_i - \underline{\lambda}_i)$ without affecting the feasibility associated with constraints (7.24) and does not increase the object function. This statement inspires us to modify the above reformulation such that constraints (7.24) are enforced if and only if $y_{ij} = 1$. Consequently, a modified robust version of the capacity planning problem (MR-CP) is presented as follows:

$$\min_{(x,y,\alpha,\beta,\gamma)} \{\sum_{j=1}^{n} c_j^f x_j + \alpha\Gamma + \sum_{j=1}^{n}\gamma_j\}$$

s.t.

$$y_{ij} \le x_j, \forall i, j$$

$$\sum_{i=1}^{m} y_{ij} \le N_j, \forall j$$

$$\sum_{j=1}^{n} y_{ij} \ge M_i, \forall i$$

$$\alpha + \zeta_{ij} \ge c_j^v(\overline{\lambda}_i - \underline{\lambda}_i)y_{ij}, \forall i, j$$

$$\sum_{i=1}^{m}\zeta_{ij} \le c_j^v(R_j x_j - \sum_{i=1}^{m}\underline{\lambda}_i y_{ij}) + \gamma_j, \forall j$$

$x_p, y_{ij} \in \{0,1\}, \forall i, j$

$\alpha \geq 0, \zeta_{ij} \geq 0, \gamma_j \geq 0, \forall i, j.$ \hfill (7.25)

Therefore, we are capable of obtaining robust solutions to the capacity planning problem by solving the mixed integer linear program (MILP) (7.25), which seeks to avoid the worst-case by imposing a limit on the level of conservativeness of the derived solution. Relative notations are intuitively interpreted as follows. First, α is viewed as the marginal value associated with the change of level of conservativeness. Second, ζ_{ij} are interpreted as the total capacity expansion in excess of the lower bound $\underline{\lambda}_i$ to fulfill order i in plant j. Third, we view γ_j as the total cost of capacity expansion associated with each plant j.

7.4 Numerical illustrations

We assume that there is no inventory of any product at the beginning of the planning period. The company headquarters choose which plants to build from among three candidate plants and then allocate four types of orders. Table 7.1 gives fixed investment required to build a plant, variable cost per unit capacity expansion and regular capacity in each plant.

The relationship between c_j^f and c_j^v indicates that 30 units of capacity expansion is equivalent to the cost of building a new plant.

Table 7.2 presents the lower and upper bounds on the uncertainty set of capacity utilization to fulfill each order i. Furthermore, we assume $M_i = 1, \forall i, N_j = 2, \forall j$.

As stated in Section 7.3, parameter Γ controls how conservative the optimal solution derived from MR-CP is. In this instance, the case $\Gamma = 0$ indicates the least conservative setting, where actual capacity utilization required to fulfill

Table 7.1 Fixed investment, variable cost per unit expansible capacity and regular capacity for each plant

Plant j	c_j^f	c_j^v	R_j
1	100	3.33	960
2	75	2.5	720
3	60	2	480

Table 7.2 Lower and upper bounds on the uncertainty set

Order i	$\underline{\lambda}_i$	$\overline{\lambda}_i$
1	300	1200
2	360	1140
3	480	1020
4	600	900

each order in a plant reaches its lower bound, while $\Gamma = 12$ implies the most conservative setting, in which case actual capacity utilization required to fulfill each order in a plant reaches its upper bound. Meanwhile, we seek to test the sensitivity of the optimal solution derived from MR-CP to the variable cost per unit expansible capacity in each plant. Table 7.3 provides different scenarios about variable cost per unit expansible capacity in each plant.

Figure 7.1 demonstrated the trend of the total fixed cost of building a plant and the variable cost associated with capacity expansion when both Γ and c_j^v change.

Table 7.3 Different scenarios with different variable costs per unit of capacity expansion in each plant

Scenarios	c_j^v		
	1	2	3
1	3.33	2.5	2
2	2.664	2	1.6
3	1.665	1.25	1
4	0.999	0.75	0.6

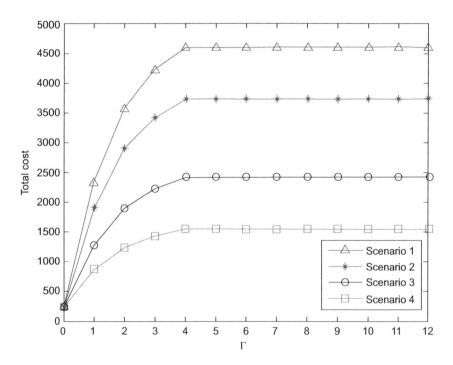

Figure 7.1 The trend of the total fixed cost required to build a plant and the variable cost of capacity expansion with respect to Γ and c_j^v

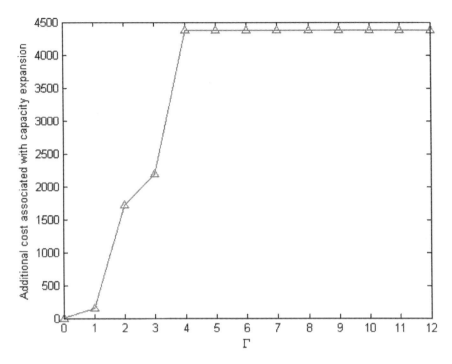

Figure 7.2 The relationship between additional costs associated with capacity expansion and the degree of conservativeness of the derived solution

As expected, the optimal objective function value increases monotonically as the level of conservativeness increases, i.e., as Γ increases, the deterioration of total cost is worse for larger unit cost of capacity expansion, i.e., when c_j^v is larger. For all scenarios, the worst-case is reached before the theoretical situation, i.e., $\Gamma = 4$ for all scenarios in this numerical illustration.

Figure 7.2 gives the relationship between additional cost associated with capacity expansion and the level of conservativeness of the derived solution.

As shown in Figure 7.2, additional cost associated with capacity expansion increases monotonically as the level of conservativeness of derived solution increases, i.e., as Γ increases. The trend demonstrates that additional cost associated with capacity expansion increases drastically when Γ increases from 4 to 5, and thereafter remains constant.

For the sake of demonstrating the effectiveness of our proposed model, we consider several different nominal values to derive optimal solutions from the deterministic version of the capacity planning problem (D-CP), and then present comparisons between these solutions and that derived from the modified robust version of capacity planning problem (MR-CP). Three instances of the nominal values of capacity utilization are given in Table 7.4.

Table 7.4 Nominal values of capacity utilization

Instances	Order i			
	1	*2*	*3*	*4*
1	525	530	615	675
2	750	700	750	750
3	975	870	885	825

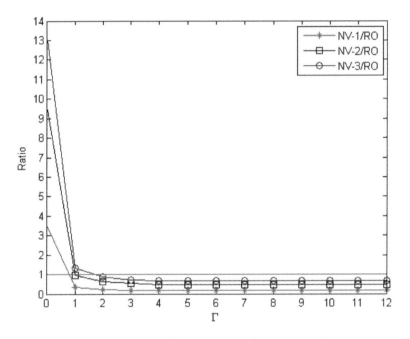

Figure 7.3 Sensitivity analysis of solution ratios with respect to Γ

To compare the solutions derived by each method, the measure of effectiveness of the proposed model is defined as the ratios that the expected cost of the D-CP derived from nominal values to the expected cost generated by our MR-CP. Figure 7.3 shows the change in solution ratios for three different nominal values referring to Scenario 1 in Table 7.3.

As shown in Figure 7.3, with the increase of Γ, the proposed MR-CP model derives poor quality solutions in all instances, and the deteriorations first increases and then keep constant. In other words, the optimal solutions remain unchanged for a given instance at a high level of Γ, i.e., for Γ ≥ 4 in Figure 7.3. For a certain level of conservativeness, high nominal value improves the quality of our MR-CP method. Moreover, for all instances, the solution when Γ = 0 performs best, where the management assigns more orders to a large capacity plant, i.e., $y_{21} = y_{41} = 1$, when $\Gamma = 0$, which definitely lowers the cost associated with capacity expansion.

7.5 Discussion

This chapter provides a modeling framework and valuable insights into the capacity planning problem faced by the manufacturing industry in the presence of demand uncertainty. We have proposed a robust optimization approach to the capacity planning problem in the face of uncertain status of capacity utilization to avoid the worst case, which: (1) does not require the exact information about the distributions, and instead profiles random variables through a polyhedral uncertainty set, (2) yields a computationally tractable mixed integer program with some auxiliary variables, and (3) allows for sensitivity analysis of the derived solutions to the level of conservativeness and variable cost of capacity expansion. The plant building decision and assignment scheme of orders to plants have been addressed with a trade-off between two competing criteria: (1) the fixed cost of building individual plants and (2) the additional cost associated with production capacity expansion across all plants. Numerical illustration has been conducted to test the effectiveness of our proposed model and provide relative analysis with respect to uncertainty.

There are ample opportunities for future research with the consideration of practical and algorithm angles. First, we can consider multiple order scheduling problems, such as integrating production planning, capacity planning and scheduling. Second, the application of algorithms to solve larger scale problems, i.e., heuristic approaches, is encouraging.

8 A case study in the Hong Kong apparel industry
Hanbo Enterprise Holdings Limited

8.1 Overview

As a one-stop solution provider of apparel supply chain management services, Hanbo Enterprise Holdings Limited was established in 1991 and offers a wide range of services, including sourcing of raw materials and third-party manufacturers, product design and development, production management, merchandising, quality control, logistics management and social compliance monitoring services, to meet customers' needs along the apparel supply chain. In this manner, Hanbo integrates the roles of importer, exporter and agent in the apparel industry. The vision of Hanbo is to help stakeholders recognize creative solutions by reducing vulnerabilities in every step of the apparel supply chain management, and the mission is to mitigate and rebalance risks associated with apparel supply chain process: Sustainability, R&D, Product Development, Sourcing, Production, QA, Logistics, Finance, IT and Talents Management. Hanbo's customers comprise mainly well-known and reputable specialty stores (including Cato Corporation, a US-based retailer of women's apparel, and a US-based specialty retailer of various products, including apparel products for young consumers), discount stores (including Target Corporation, a large US-based discount store operator) and department stores (including some of the largest US-based department store operators which rank amongst the top five retailers in the US by revenue and which have flagship stores in New York). To minimize manufacturing and labour costs, we have ceased taking orders for our own in-house production of apparel products at the Contract Processing Factory since April 2012 and also outsourced the labour-intensive manufacturing function to various third-party manufacturers located mainly in Cambodia, Bangladesh and the PRC. This allows us to focus our resources on the provision of apparel supply chain management services to our customers.

The following is a summary of the key milestones in the development of Hanbo's business:

Year	Event
1991	Hanbo Enterprises HK was established in Hong Kong to carry on the business of manufacturing and trading of apparel products in Hong Kong. Opened its office in Hong Kong.
1996	Began to gradually change the nature of its business to become an apparel supply chain manager.

2001	Began to engage third-party manufacturers in Cambodia for the production of woven wear. Began to engage third-party manufacturers in Kenya for the production of woven wear (ceased such engagements prior to the commencement of the Track Record Period).
2003	Began to engage third-party manufacturers in Sri Lanka for the production of woven wear (ceased such engagements prior to the commencement of the Track Record Period).
2005	Opened its office in Macao.
2006	The Contract Processing Factory was established in Shenzhen.
2007	Opened its office in Shenzhen.
2010	Began to engage third-party manufacturers in Bangladesh for the production of woven wear. The Board made a strategic decision to gradually cease all of its own in-house production and focus its resources on the provision of apparel supply chain management services.
2011	Opened its liaison office in Bangladesh.
2012	Ceased taking orders for its own in-house production of apparel products at the Contract Processing Factory.
2013	Opened its office in Cambodia.

Hanbo proposes a **SMART** supply chain business model for the stakeholders along the apparel supply chain. More specifically,

1 **S** denotes *Streamlined*: effectively simplify the supply chain by replacing the roles of importers, exporters and agencies, and clear obstacles to order/ production flow to reduce lead times;
2 **M** denotes *Measurable*: set up standards and goals, provide reports such as customer, mill and factory score cards to measure the performance of supply chain partners;
3 **A** denotes *Aligned*: align with factories, suppliers and customers to receive updated customer demand information and plan accordingly, coordinate workflow of development, production and procurement to achieve optimal efficiency and set congruent incentives aimed at reducing total supply chain costs;
4 **R** denotes *Resilient*: show agility in responding to dynamic markets to gain or maintain competitive advantage;
5 **T** denotes *Transparent*: develop ERP system to improve planning and visibility of total supply chain costs, share information with suppliers and customers to become more efficient and competitive and set up first sale program to help customer reduce import duties.

In a word, Hanbo, a one-stop apparel supply chain solution provider, strives to mitigate risks in the whole supply chain process, such as price, quality, quantity, delivery and compliance. Hanbo aims to provide solutions to improve supply chain sustainability, transparency and visibility.

Nowadays, Hanbo Enterprises Holdings Limited and its subsidiaries are principally engaged in (1) apparel trading and supply chain management services business; (2) financial services business; (3) money lending business; and (4) securities investment during the period.

8.2   Business model

At the start of each main fashion season (i.e. Spring/Summer or Autumn/Winter) and from time to time, we would make presentations to our customers on product designs which we have developed and suitable raw materials. When we receive an indication from a customer that it would like to place an order with us, if the customer has already created product designs for the apparel products which it would like us to procure for them, then the customer would provide us with a technical specifications package for specific apparel products. Staff from our merchandising department and other relevant departments would then meet with our customer's product design team to discuss the technical specifications package, and we would provide suggestions in relation to the composition of the apparel products. If a customer has not itself created any product designs for the apparel products which it would like us to procure for them, then our product design and development department would meet with the customer to discuss their requirements for the product designs for apparel products that they would like us to procure for them, and we would provide research and development services and suggested product designs to the customer.

After the product designs are finalized, staff from our merchandising department would then discuss with our customer a merchandising programme based on our customer's requirements as to product designs and raw materials required. We would then, based on the finalized product designs, produce product samples in our sample room(s) located in Shenzhen and/or Phnom Penh, Cambodia and deliver these product samples to our customer for their consideration. After that, we would provide an initial price quotation for the apparel products and the estimated schedule for delivery of the apparel products to our customer. We would also perfect the fit, style and function of the product samples so that they comply with our customer's requirements and specifications. Once our customer is satisfied with, and grants their approval of, the product samples, they would confirm the quantity of apparel products required, and we would then finalize the price of the apparel products with our customer. Our customer would then place their order with us for the apparel products they requires We would then engage a third-party manufacturer in either Cambodia, Bangladesh or the PRC to produce such apparel products. We, or we (on behalf of the third-party manufacturer), or the third-party manufacturer itself, would place orders with raw material suppliers for the procurement of suitable raw materials to cater to our customer's needs. Staff from our production and quality control department would provide technical support to the third-party manufacturers; carry out interim inspections of semi-finished apparel products at various stages of the manufacturing process; and then carry out a final inspection on the finished apparel products after the manufacturing process is completed, but before the finished products are delivered to our customers' designated warehouses or designated shipping points.

Figure 8.1 illustrates Hanbo's business model for the provision of the apparel supply chain management services.

8.2.1 Sourcing of orders

During the Track Record Period, Hanbo generally obtained the orders through (1) liaising directly with representative(s) from the headquarters of the existing customers or potential customers and took orders from them; or (2) liaising directly with the relevant sourcing agent engaged by one of Hanbo's customers and took orders from the representative(s) from the headquarters of the customer.

8.2.2 Sourcing of materials

During the Track Record Period, the raw materials (including fabric, buttons, threads and zippers) used in the manufacture of the apparel products we procured for Hanbo's customers were mainly sourced from suppliers based in the PRC and Hong Kong. Hanbo, on behalf of the third-party manufacturer, or the third-party manufacturer itself would source suitable raw materials (such as fabric, buttons, threads and zippers) from suppliers which are either recommended by us or nominated by Hanbo's customers. Typically, the third-party manufacturers would source the raw materials directly from the raw materials suppliers. However, if a large amount of raw materials are required for a particular order from a customer and a third-party manufacturer does not have the financial resources to purchase those raw materials, Hanbo (on behalf of the third-party manufacturer) would purchase the required raw materials.

8.2.3 Production management

Instead of being heavily involved in the actual production process of the apparel products, Hanbo has ceased taking orders for its own in-house production of apparel products at the Contract Processing Factory since April 2012 and also outsourced the labour-intensive manufacturing function to various third-party manufacturers located mainly in Cambodia, Bangladesh and the PRC. As such, in terms of the production process of apparel products, Hanbo mainly manages and monitors the overall production process of the apparel products. Hanbo's production management services include the procurement of suitable raw materials and the inspection of the quality of raw materials; the selection of suitable third-party manufacturers and overseeing the performance of the third-party manufacturers; and the coordination of the apparel supply chain management services that it provides.

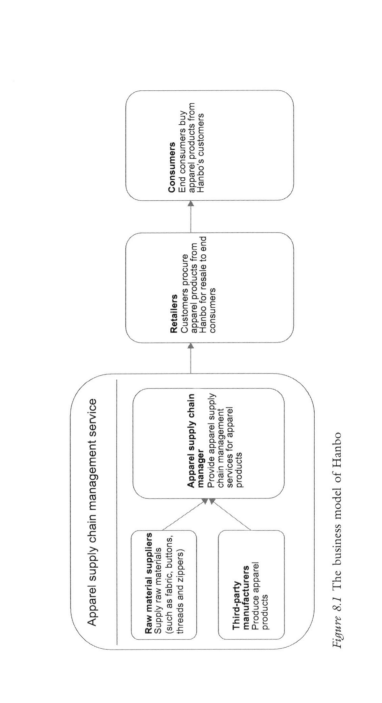

Figure 8.1 The business model of Hanbo

As Hanbo does not enter into long-term contracts with third-party manufacturers, our costs of production may increase if our third-party manufacturers
increase their subcontracting fees, which Hanbo may not be able to pass along
to its customers. For the associated risks, Hanbo is dependent on third-party
manufacturers for the production of apparel products, so disruption in our
relationship with them or their manufacturing operations could adversely affect
our apparel supply chain management services.

8.2.4 Pricing strategy

The apparel products are priced separately for each order based on the estimated
cost of, and/or the suggested merchandise price for, a product. Hanbo agrees
upon the prices of the apparel products with its customers after the product
designs are finalized and the product samples have been approved by its customers.
The apparel products are price sensitive in the sense that the agreed upon prices
will usually not be adjusted even if, subsequently, there are changes to the price
of the raw materials Hanbo sources from its suppliers or the prices of finished
apparel products manufactured by the third-party manufacturers, or changes to
the subcontracting fees charged by the third-party manufacturers. In determining
the estimated cost of the apparel product, Hanbo estimates the associated product
design and development costs and subcontracting fees. When determining final
price for an apparel product, Hanbo would consider a number of other factors
such as the size of the relevant order, the type of the apparel product, its relationship with the relevant customer and the timing for delivery.

Hanbo's sales are subject to seasonal fluctuations and are largely determined in
part by two major fashion seasons: Spring/Summer and Autumn/Winter. Hanbo
generally record higher sales from December to April as its customers have higher
demand for woven wear products for their Spring/Summer collections.

8.3 Customers and suppliers

8.3.1 Customers

Hanbo's customers comprise mainly well-known and reputable specialty stores
(including Cato Corporation, a US-based retailer of women's apparel, and a
US-based specialty retailer of various products, including apparel products for
young consumers), discount stores (including Target Corporation, a US-based
large discount store operator) and department stores (including some of the
largest US-based department store operators which rank amongst the top five
retailers in the US by revenue and which have flagship stores in New York).
Hanbo has maintained business relationships with our top five customers for
six to 14 years. Hanbo had a customer base of 24, 20 and 15 customers as of
31 December 2011, 2012 and 2013 respectively. Hanbo has developed a
concentrated customer base as a result of its strategy to place a stronger focus
on core customers from whom it expects to generate a substantial amount of

gross profits on recurring basis and to allocate resources on a target group of customers so as to benefit from economies of scale.

Hanbo's sales to its top five customers accounted for approximately 88.7 percent, 84.9 percent and 84.8 percent of its total revenue as of 31 December 2011, 2012 and 2013 respectively. Hanbo's sales to its largest customer accounted for approximately 28.8 percent, 33.8 percent and 29.3 percent of its total revenue as of 31 December 2011, 2012 and 2013 respectively. Sales to its top five customers represented approximately 88.7 percent, 84.9 percent and 84.8 percent of its total sales and accounted for approximately 82.3 percent, 78.8 percent and 80.4 percent of its gross trade and bills receivables balances as of 31 December 2011, 2012 and 2013 respectively. If its customers were to terminate their respective relationships with Hanbo entirely, or if there was a change in their creditworthiness, Hanbo's business would be adversely affected.

8.3.2   Suppliers

Hanbo's suppliers consist of (1) third-party manufacturers that manufacture apparel products for its customers and (2) suppliers of raw materials (such as fabric, buttons, threads and zippers). Hanbo has cooperated with top five suppliers for over three years., Hanbo engaged over 35, 30 and 20 third-party manufacturers and over 185, 175 and 145 suppliers of raw materials as of 31 December 2011, 2012 and 2013 respectively. Hanbo believes its relatively concentrated supplier base allows it to reap the benefits of economies of scale and to focus its resources on maintaining steady relationships with the main suppliers. Hanbo also believes this does not pose significant risk to its business, given the abundance of suppliers in the market and its operational flexibility as an apparel supply chain manager which would allow it to source and cooperate with alternative suppliers in a timely manner should the need occur.

Hanbo's five largest suppliers, comprising third-party manufacturers, accounted for approximately 59.9 percent, 58.8 percent and 65.0 percent of its total cost of sales as of 31 December 2011, 2012 and 2013 respectively. Its largest supplier, a third-party manufacturer, accounted for approximately 22.1 percent, 13.8 percent and 15.9 percent of the total cost of sales as of 31 December 2011, 2012 and 2013 respectively.

8.4   Competitive landscape

The apparel supply chain management service provider industry in the Greater China region is highly fragmented, with more than 482 and 516 service providers in 2012 and 2013 respectively. The top ten apparel supply chain management service providers accounted for about HK$139.9 billion, representing approximately 49.3 percent, of the total market revenue of the apparel supply chain management service industry in 2012.

8.4.1 Competitive strengths of Hanbo

Hanbo believes that it has the following competitive strengths:

1   *One-stop solution provider of apparel supply chain management services.* We act as a one-stop solution provider of apparel supply chain management services for woven wear to our customers. By engaging us as their apparel supply chain manager, our customers can rely on us to meet their needs along the apparel supply chain. Our Directors believe that this is more cost-effective and efficient for our customers, as our customers do not have to separately engage service providers for the services required for each step in the apparel supply chain which may be more time-consuming and costly. As a majority of our Executive Directors have extensive experience in the apparel industry (including the aspects involved in each step of the apparel supply chain, including sourcing of raw materials and apparel production), our Executive Directors know the needs of our customers and how to meet their needs through the provision of our apparel supply chain management services. Our apparel supply chain management services include sourcing of raw materials and third-party manufacturers, sample creation, product design and development, production management, merchandising, quality control, logistics management and social compliance monitoring services. Based on our staff's knowledge of fabrics in our fabric department and the business relationships we have developed with raw materials suppliers, we are able to source raw materials of acceptable quality from raw materials suppliers in a manner that our Directors believe is cost-efficient for our customers. Staff in our product design and development department or merchandising department play an active role in making suggestions to our customers as to the types of fabric and other raw materials that could be used to manufacture apparel products based on any requirements our customers may have (including their target price for the apparel products), fashion trends, consumer preferences and the efficiency of the production of the apparel products by third-party manufacturers. If our customer considers that the price of a particular raw material stipulated by a supplier (whether or not the supplier is nominated by the customer) is exorbitant or if a particular raw material is not readily available, we may suggest an alternative supplier (as selected from our extensive portfolio of over 673 raw material suppliers [as of the Latest Practicable Date]) to our customer for its consideration and approval. With the strong talent and skills of the staff in our product design and development department, we have been able to provide our customers with product designs incorporating fashionable trends and styles to cater to our customers' needs or provide design inspiration to our customers. We have also been able to produce product samples for our customers based on our customers' preferred product designs. Based on the extensive knowledge of our staff in our merchandising department regarding the local environment of locations where the

third-party manufacturers we engage are based, and our experience in dealing with third-party manufacturers in Cambodia, Bangladesh and the PRC, we have been able to allocate our customers' orders to third-party manufacturers in a manner that is cost-effective and efficient for our customers. Further, as our third-party manufacturers are located in different countries, interruptions to production schedules for a customer's order due to country-specific event(s) (such as the closure of production facilities over a public holiday period in a particular country, or workers' strikes in a particular country) could be kept to a minimum, as our Directors believe that we could allocate customer's order to a third-party manufacturer in another country where such event(s) are not, at that time, occurring. This could help us to ensure that our customers' orders could be delivered on time

2   *Effective monitoring and control of the provision of our apparel supply chain management services through the use of our ERP system.* We have developed our own proprietary ERP system through which we effectively monitor and control the provision of our apparel supply chain management services. Our ERP system is a vital component of our operations and facilitates the operation and integration of our different business functions by enhancing communication and information flow. We recognize that as our Group grows, our ERP system will have to evolve at the same time. We have a dedicated team who monitor our ERP system on a quarterly basis and make the necessary upgrades to improve our ERP system's functionality and relevance to our business operations. With our ERP system, we can also manage and review not only our customers' current order status, but also data relating to our customers' order history for our apparel supply chain management services, and our financial data on a centralized system which is used by all of our departments in all of our offices, rather than having isolated software applications in each department that cannot interface with any other system. Our ERP system is used throughout our apparel supply chain management process. Each stage is recorded on our ERP system so that our management team and staff have ready access to information relating to our business operations. This allows our managers to view progress reports on each customer's orders and to access monthly reports on not only orders completed, but also on the status of uncompleted orders and unpaid invoices, and whether each stage of the apparel supply chain has been completed according to the relevant prescribed schedule. As a result, we are able to respond to enquiries from our customers on the status of their respective orders on a timely basis, which we believe is essential to enhance our customers' experience in using our apparel supply chain management services. Another useful feature of our ERP system is the ability to compare information on the system, such as the track record of our suppliers' performance, lead times for different orders, the efficiency and reliability of third-party manufacturers to meet orders on time and customer feedback. We believe this allows our management to make more informed decisions in terms of

cost estimates, lead times and selection of suppliers and third-party manu-facturers so that we can provide more effective apparel supply chain manage-ment services to our customers. In addition, we are willing to share the information on the track record of our suppliers' performance with our customers so that our customers are kept informed of the standards of performance of our suppliers. We are constantly upgrading our information systems, which we believe would enhance our operations and profitability.

3   *Stringent quality assurance and control measures.* We have adopted stringent quality assurance and control measures to ensure that the apparel products we procure for our customers are of high quality. Our quality control staff are involved in each material stage of the apparel supply chain from inspect-ing product samples before they are delivered to our customers for their consideration, to inspecting raw materials procured from suppliers, to per-forming checks and assessments on-site at the manufacturing facilities of the third-party manufacturers during each material stage of the production process, and to inspecting the finished apparel products before they are delivered to our customers' designated warehouses or designated shipping points. These inspections, checks and assessments are performed to ensure that the raw materials used in the manufacture of the apparel products and the finished apparel products themselves fully comply with our customers' requirements and any applicable standards for apparel products. As of the Latest Practicable Date, our production and quality control department comprised 29 staff stationed in Hong Kong, Cambodia, Bangladesh and Shenzhen. Our production and quality control department is fully conversant with the latest quality standards (such as the AQL standard and the Four-Point System) applicable to apparel products and the raw materials procured for the production of apparel products. The AQL standard refers to the maximum number of defects that could be considered acceptable during the random sampling of an inspection. The Four-Point System refers to a pro-cedure to establish a numerical designation for the grading of fabrics based on a visual inspection of the fabrics. We have quality control staff stationed in every location where we engage third-party manufacturers to produce apparel products. Our quality control staff work closely with the third-party manufacturers and monitor each stage of the manufacturing process. As the quality of raw materials (in particular, fabric) procured from suppliers for the manufacture of apparel products and the quality control standards and measures adopted by the third-party manufacturers play an important role in the quality of the finished apparel product, we conduct detailed evalua-tions of our fabric suppliers and third-party manufacturers. We evaluate and select our fabric suppliers and third-party manufacturers based on their experience in the apparel industry, reputation, technical capabilities, financial strength, production capacity, quality control effectiveness, ethical practices and record of compliance with applicable standards for apparel products. Building the trust and confidence of our customers is of paramount impor-tance to us, and we believe that by having a high standard for the quality

of the apparel products that we procure for our customers, we are able to maintain the trust and confidence of our customers.

4   *Experienced management team with extensive industry experience.*

8.5   Business strategies

Hanbo aims to maintain its growth in the apparel supply chain management services market and enhance our overall competitiveness and market share. Hanbo intends to achieve its objectives by adopting the following key business strategies:

1   *Expand Hanbo's product types to further cater to its customers' needs and attract new customers.* With the aim to further cater to our customers' needs by providing more comprehensive service solutions to our customers and to attract new customers, we intend to broaden our existing woven wear product offerings and expand our product types to include cut-and-sewn knitwear. To increase our market share in the cut-and-sewn knitwear market, our Directors believe that we need to further develop our product design capabilities in the area of cut-and-sewn knitwear and expand our base of suppliers to include more suppliers of raw materials used in the production of cut-and-sewn knitwear. We intend to develop a comprehensive range of cut-and-sewn knitwear (including tops and bottoms) for all genres of the public with the help and skills of our experienced product design and development department. Our Directors believe that by expanding the types of products we offer to include cut-and-sewn knitwear, we would be able to offer cut-and-sewn knitwear to our existing customers and potential new customers that may be engaged in the sale of cut-and-sewn knitwear to end consumers. We would also be able to increase our coverage of the apparel market, in particular, the men's and women's winter apparel market. In addition, by leveraging our network of third-party manufacturers in Cambodia and Bangladesh, our experience in dealing with third-party manufacturers and our capabilities in providing apparel supply chain management services to meet the needs of our customers along the apparel supply chain, we intend to attract new customers in the PRC market which traditionally may have only engaged manufacturers in the PRC (and not elsewhere) to manufacture their products and which may be engaging various service providers separately for the services required for each step in the apparel supply chain instead of employing the use of a one-stop apparel supply chain manager.

2   *Further enhance Hanbo's information technology systems and upgrade its ERP system.* We plan to continue to improve our ERP system through our dedicated team who monitor our ERP system and make the necessary upgrades to improve our ERP system's functionality and relevance to our business operations. We effectively monitor and control the provision of our apparel supply chain management services through our own self-developed ERP

system. As our business continues to expand and to improve the efficiency and effectiveness of our apparel supply chain management services, we plan to invest in enhancing our ERP system by (1) upgrading the software we use; (2) enhancing certain features of our ERP such as those relating to cost controls on each order and monitoring the progress of each order; and (3) developing new features such as a mobile application which would provide increased accessibility to our ERP system from a wider range of portable electronic devices so that the progress of orders can be monitored by our staff or customers from a location away from our offices. This new mobile application will primarily be used by our own staff so that they can better manage their designated orders, but we also plan to enable our customers to track their orders on our ERP system through the use of such mobile application.

3 *Expand the geographical base of the third-party manufacturers.* During the Track Record Period, we engaged 32 third-party manufacturers on average each year which are located mainly in Cambodia, Bangladesh and the PRC. We are exploring the possibility of engaging third-party manufacturers in Vietnam and Indonesia. As of the Latest Practicable Date, we have only placed purchase orders with third-party manufacturers in Vietnam and Indonesia on a trial order basis for a minimal quantity of apparel products to assess and evaluate the quality and properties of such apparel products. As of the Latest Practicable Date, we have not formally engaged any third-party manufacturer in Vietnam or Indonesia. In addition, we intend to, from time to time, explore the possibility of engaging third-party manufacturers in other countries where overall costs (including manufacturing costs) may be low and government incentives may be offered to market players in the apparel industry, as this may in turn help to lower the costs of manufacturing apparel products and hence, make the pricing of apparel products more attractive to our customers. Our Directors believe that by expanding our geographical base of third-party manufacturers we would be able to provide our customers with a wider range of choices as to where apparel products may be manufactured. We would also enjoy increased flexibility in terms of our choice of a suitable third-party manufacturer to manufacture the apparel products. As public holiday periods vary between different countries, diversifying our geographical base of third-party manufacturers would also help to ensure that interruptions in production schedules for a customer's order due to the closure of production facilities over a public holiday period in a particular country are kept to a minimum, as we would be able to allocate that customer's order to a third-party manufacturer in another country where that public holiday period does not apply. When evaluating whether to engage a new third-party manufacturer, we will take into account certain factors, including its experience in the apparel industry, reputation, technical capabilities, financial strength, production capacity, quality control effectiveness, ethical practices and record of compliance with applicable standards for apparel products.

4   *Further develop its design and development capabilities.* We consider the experience and in-depth industry knowledge of our product design and development department to be a key factor in our business. To further enhance our design and development capabilities, we intend to recruit additional staff who have the requisite experience and ability to design and develop both enhanced product designs for apparel products and new and fresh product designs that can be added to our range of product offerings. We also plan to offer relevant training to the staff in our product design and development department so that they can further develop their product design skills.

8.6   Risk factors

There are certain risks involved in Hanbo's operations and in connection with the Global Offering, many of which are beyond its control. These risks can be broadly categorized into: (1) risks relating to Hanbo's business; (2) risks relating to apparel industry; (3) risks relating to conducting business in the PRC; (4) risks relating to conducting business in countries other than the PRC; and (5) risks relating to the Global Offering.

8.6.1   *Risks relating to Hanbo's business*

Set forth below are some of the major risks that may materially and adversely affect us:

1   Aggregate sales to Hanbo's top five customers represented approximately 88.7 percent, 84.9 percent and 84.8 percent of its total sales and accounted for approximately 82.3 percent, 78.8 percent and 80.4 percent of its gross trade and bills receivables balances as of 31 December 2011, 2012 and 2013 respectively. If Hanbo's customers were to terminate their respective relationships with us entirely, or if there was a change in their creditworthiness, our business would be adversely affected. The top five customers are not obligated to continue placing orders with us at all or at the same level that they historically have done, and Hanbo can offer no assurances that they will do so. If there is any unexpected cessation of, or substantial reduction in the volume of, orders with any of the top five customers, Hanbo can offer no assurances that it would be able to obtain replacement of orders to cover any such drop in sales in a timely manner or that, if Hanbo was able to obtain other orders, they would be on commercially reasonable terms. In addition, if any of our customers fail to settle the sales proceeds in accordance with the agreed credit terms, Hanbo's working capital position may be adversely affected. Bad debt provisions or write-offs may also be required for receivables, which will have an adverse effect on our profitability. If any of the relationships with our customers were to be so altered, and Hanbo was unable to obtain replacement orders, or if there is a change

in its customers' creditworthiness, our results of operations would be adversely affected.

2 During the Track Record Period, the US was Hanbo's largest market based on the geographical destination of shipment of apparel products procured for its customers during such period. Aggregate sales to Hanbo's largest market, the US, accounted for approximately 91.0 percent, 90.4 percent and 88.6 percent of its total sales as of 31 December 2011, 2012 and 2013 respectively. If there was a drastic decrease in orders from its customers in the US, Hanbo cannot guarantee that it would be able to make up the loss of sales from other markets. This would adversely affect the business operations and financial results.

3 Hanbo is dependent on third-party manufacturers for the production of apparel products, so disruption to our relationship with them or their manufacturing operations could adversely affect the apparel supply chain management services. Almost all of the apparel products we sourced for Hanbo's customers during the Track Record Period were sourced from third-party manufacturers. The number of apparel products produced by third-party manufacturers accounted for 95.0 percent, 97.8 percent and 100.0 percent of the total apparel products procured through our services as of 31 December 2011, 2012 and 2013 respectively. Hence, the reliability and efficiency of third-party manufacturers play an important part in our apparel supply chain management services. However, we do not enter into long-term contracts with any of our third-party manufacturers. There is no assurance that all of our third-party manufacturers will continue to be able or willing to supply apparel products to us at our desired quality, in a timely manner and on commercially acceptable terms. If any of our major third-party manufacturers should terminate their business relationship with us or if there are changes to the current arrangements, we may not be able to source suitable products from comparable alternative third-party manufacturers in a timely manner or on commercially reasonable terms. This could result in a delay in the production schedule and affect adversely our ability to fulfil customers' orders and in turn adversely affect our sales and gross profit margin rates. Without any long-term contract, the terms of services provided by our third-party manufacturers may also be susceptible to fluctuations with regard to pricing, timing and quality. For example, if our third-party manufacturers increase their subcontracting fees due to factors, such as an increase in their operating costs resulting from an increase in prices of raw materials or an increase in labour wages, we may incur significant costs which we may not be able to pass along to our customers, or we may need to adjust our operations, which may strain our financial and management resources. Further, the stability of operations and performance of our third-party manufacturers will also affect us. If there is any disruption to the third-party manufacturers' operations from natural or other causes, such as weather, natural disaster, fire or other technical and mechanical difficulties, then their production schedule could be delayed. Any damage to the third-party

manufacturers' production facilities could be costly and time consuming to repair and could delay the production of apparel products and cause knock-on delays in our delivery schedules and impair our ability to adequately fulfil our customers' orders, which could adversely affect our apparel supply chain management services. If any of the products they manufacture cannot satisfy our customers' required standards or have to be returned for any reason, we may not be able to meet our commitments to our customers, which may have an adverse impact on our business reputation. We may also incur significant additional costs that we may not be able to pass along to our customers, which in turn could have a material adverse effect on our business, financial condition and results of operations. If we discover that an existing third-party manufacturer has any material non-compliance issues, for instance, violations of trade laws and health and safety regulations, we will need to divert management and financial resources and incur additional costs in liaising and following up with that third-party manufacturer on rectifying the non-compliance and consider whether to cease our business relationship with that third-party manufacturer. In the event of termination of, or changes to, the current arrangements with the third-party manufacturers for any reason, our Group may not be able to locate comparable alternative manufacturers that could provide manufacturing services in a timely manner and/or on commercially acceptable terms. This could result in a delay in the production schedule and in turn adversely affect our Group's business operations and financial results.

4　Any failure to maintain an effective quality management system may have a material adverse effect on Hanbo's reputation, operations and financial condition. As an apparel supply chain service provider, Hanbo relies on its internal quality control system to ensure the levels of quality in different areas of its services. If there is any significant failure or deterioration of our quality management system or if we fail to meet or conform to the required specifications of our customers, such failure and any subsequent negative publicity could result in the loss of sales, which could have a material adverse effect on its business reputation, results of operations and financial condition.

5　The business is subject to risks related to extreme changes in weather conditions. Changes in weather conditions will impact consumers' purchasing power and needs. Certain extreme and unpredictable weather patterns may affect consumer spending and preferences and the choice of products they seek in response to weather changes and other disruptive events. We, as an apparel supply chain service provider, and our customers are accustomed to traditional seasonal cycles and the apparel products we procure for our customers may not adapt to distinct changes between seasons or in weather conditions. For example, if the apparel products are not suitable to accommodate inclement or unfavorable weather conditions, the sales volume of our customers may drop. Also, weather events may affect consumer purchasing priorities and household spending patterns. For example, consumers may spend more on products that help them adapt to weather conditions, or on energy, which may reduce their spending on apparel products and in turn negatively impact our sales. If we fail to adapt to new seasonality trends or consumer spending behavior, our revenue and business conditions may be adversely affected.

6 Strikes and other disruptive events may adversely affect Hanbo's operations. We have operations in Cambodia where strikes have occurred recently. Strikes and other disruptive events beyond our control, such as changes in political environment, whether in Cambodia or other countries where we have operations, may disrupt and delay transportation of materials and finished products. We may have to increase extra costs, such as transportation costs, to ensure that our production and delivery schedules are met. If we fail to meet the delivery timelines under our customers' orders, we may need to compensate our customers, and our customers may lose confidence in us. Significant increase in our costs could result in a diversion of resources and could substantially harm our operating results.

7 Hanbo generates a majority of our revenue from Hanbo Enterprises Macao, where Hanbo currently enjoys tax exemptions in Macao. However, Hanbo cannot guarantee that it will continue to do so in the future if there are changes in legislation in Macao. If there are disputes arising over the amount of our tax filings or changes to legislation, interpretation or practices by tax authorities in any jurisdiction in which it has business operations, our tax liabilities could increase and this may have an adverse effect on our cash flow and financial conditions. We enjoyed tax exemptions in Macao during the Track Record Period. A majority of our revenue was generated from Hanbo Enterprises Macao during the Track Record Period and such revenue was exempted from Macao complementary tax under the current Macao Offshore Law. For details, see "Regulations – Regulatory requirements in Macao – Tax exemption". However, we cannot assure that we will continue to enjoy such tax exemptions in the future if there are changes to Macao law, regulations and policies, and we may be subject to tax. Similarly, we cannot assure that the tax laws, regulations, policies, practices or interpretation of other jurisdictions applicable to us will not change. Such changes may cause us to pay a higher rate of tax or face restrictions in our business operations in those jurisdictions. In any of these jurisdictions, the local authority or other parties may dispute the amount of our tax filings. We may find that any changes or disputes are implemented or raised against us quickly and with little warning. If we cannot mitigate for the increase in our tax liabilities then there could be an adverse effect on our cash flow and financial conditions.

8 Tax authorities could challenge our allocation of taxable income which could increase our overall tax liability. During the Track Record Period, Hanbo Enterprises HK and Yibao Clothing both provided supply chain support services to Hanbo Enterprises Macao. The relevant service fee income received by Hanbo Enterprises HK has been reported for Hong Kong profits tax, and the service fee received by Yibao Clothing has been

reported for relevant PRC taxes authorities (including income tax and turnover taxes). Our Directors, having made reasonable enquiries, consider that the cost-plus methodology to determine the service fee received by Hanbo Enterprises HK is supported by appropriate transfer pricing analysis, and they confirm that Yibao Clothing is remunerated on a cost-plus basis for the services provided. However, our determination of tax liability is always subject to review or examination by authorities in various jurisdictions. There can be no assurance that tax authorities reviewing such arrangements would not challenge the appropriateness of our transfer pricing arrangement, or that any relevant laws governing such arrangements will not be modified. In the event that an authority of any relevant jurisdiction finds that transfer prices and terms we have applied are not appropriate, such authority could require our relevant subsidiaries to re-determine transfer prices and thereby reallocate the income or adjust the taxable income. Any such reallocation or adjustment could result in a higher overall tax liability for us and adversely affect our business, financial condition and results of operations.

9   Hanbo is exposed to currency exchange rate fluctuations because we receive a majority of our revenue in US dollars, but we incur many of our expenses in other currencies. Future exchange rate fluctuations between the US dollar and other currencies may adversely affect our business. As most of our sales are made in the US, most of our revenue is denominated in US dollars. However, we pay some of the third-party manufacturers and some of our staff based on the relevant local currency. We incur and settle such costs in Hong Kong dollars, MOP, RMB or BDT. We have not entered into any agreements to hedge our exchange rate exposure relating to any of these currencies and there is no assurance that we will be able to enter into such agreements on commercially viable terms in the future. We are therefore vulnerable to US dollar depreciation and MOP, RMB or BDT appreciation. Accordingly, we can offer no assurances that future exchange rate fluctuations between the US dollar and other currencies will not adversely affect our business.

10 Hanbo generally does not have long-term agreements with our customers, and therefore, they have no commitment to place future orders with us, which exposes us to the risk of uncertainty and potential volatility with respect to our revenue. Purchases are typically made on an order-by-order basis with no commitment for the customer to place further orders with us. Consequently, most of our customers, including our top five customers, may cancel, reduce or defer future orders at will. The volume of our customers' orders and our product offerings may vary significantly from period to period, and it is difficult for us to forecast future order quantities. We offer no assurances that any of our customers will continue to place orders with us in the future at the same level as in the current or prior periods, or even at all. Furthermore, the actual volume of our customers' orders may be inconsistent with our expectations at the time that we plan our

expenditures. As a result, our business operations, financial condition and results of operations may vary from period to period and may fluctuate significantly in the future. If any or a number of our customers were to cease placing orders with us, without sufficient time for us to obtain alternative orders, our results of operations would be adversely affected. We experienced an increase in revenue for the year ended 31 December 2013 of approximately 19.6 percent comparing to the year ended 31 December 2012, and such an increase was mainly attributable to the increase in revenue from our top customer in 2013, who had increased their orders by approximately HK$91.9 million as a result of their new business direction. We have no control over our customer's business development plans, and we cannot assure that such customer will continue to adopt a business strategy that would result in increased orders placed with us. We have not entered into a long-term agreement with contractual commitment on the part of such a customer to place future orders with this customer. There is no guarantee that our relationship with this customer will not deteriorate. We cannot assure you that this customer will continue to place orders with us at current levels on similar terms, or at all. If this customer significantly reduces its orders placed with us or ceases its business relationship with us, and we fail to compensate for the decrease by increasing sales to other customers, or bring in new customers to generate comparable sales volumes, then our business, results of operations and financial performance could be adversely affected.

11 A material disruption of our information technology systems could adversely affect our supply chain management services. Our ability to fulfil orders from our customers is dependent on the efficient, proper and uninterrupted operations at our facilities. We rely on our information technology systems, particularly our ERP, to effectively manage our apparel supply chain management service operations, including customers and suppliers information, order entry, order fulfillment and other administrative processes. Our information technology systems may be vulnerable to damage or interruption from circumstances beyond our control, including fire, natural disaster, systems failures, security breaches or viruses. Any such damage or interruption could have an adverse effect on our business and prevent us from paying our suppliers, the third-party manufacturers or employees, or receiving payments from our customers, or performing other services required by our business on a timely basis. The failure of our information technology systems to perform to our expectations could disrupt our business and may require us to make unplanned capital expenditures. This would adversely affect our business, financial condition and the efficiency of our apparel supply chain management services.

12 Some of Hanbo's customers are sensitive to social responsibility and social compliance standards. If we or the third-party manufacturers have or are perceived to have failed to comply with these standards, our reputation could be adversely affected and customers may choose not to continue their

businesses with us. The customers are facing increasing pressure to ensure that labour practices and factory conditions in relation to their products meet certain social responsibility standards. Accordingly, a number of our customers require their suppliers to fulfil their own corporate social responsibility standards or those set out under independent programmes such as SA 8000 standard. There can be no assurance that we will discover violations of social responsibility and social compliance standards by the third-party manufacturers in a timely manner. If any of the third-party manufacturers fail to remedy a violation, we may cease to allocate orders to them and may be required to re-direct unfulfilled orders to other third-party manufacturers, which could delay our supply chain services and increase our costs and consequently, reduce profitability. We could also experience significant damage to our reputation, and affected customers may discontinue our services which could adversely affect our business.

13 Fluctuations in the price, availability and quality of raw materials could result in increased costs for Hanbo. As sourcing raw materials for our customers is part of our apparel supply chain services, our business is dependent on our ability to source sufficient supplies of raw materials that meet our quality requirements at satisfactory prices and in a timely manner. For our costs incurred in relation to raw materials during the Track Record Period, see "Financial Information – Cost of sales". The availability of raw materials may be affected by many factors beyond our control, including natural disasters such as droughts, floods and earthquakes, seasonal fluctuations, climate conditions, economic conditions, customer demand and governmental regulations. A material shortage in the supply of raw materials will affect production and delivery schedules and customer's perception of our sourcing ability. Raw material suppliers may take into account many factors, such as demand and supply when fixing the prices of their raw materials. Increases in raw material prices will increase our needs for working capital and financing, cause a drop in sales and affect our gross profit margin. The apparel industry saw a sudden increase in the price of cotton in 2010 and 2011. The unexpected increase in cotton price in 2011 affected our gross profit margin of 2011.

14 The business performance depends on Hanbo's ability to retain the services of our senior management and key personnel, and any failure in retaining any one of them may adversely affect our financial condition and results of operations. Our business performance depends, to a significant extent, on the continued services and the performance of the senior members of our management team, who have substantial management and operational experience in the apparel industry. Our Directors believe that these persons possess the relevant knowledge, experience and skills, especially in their familiarity with our business and substantial expertise in apparel supply chain management services. They are therefore essential to us in carrying out our business and future plans. We can offer no assurances that the services of our senior management team can be retained. We have not subscribed for

key-man life or similar insurance covering our senior management. If we lose the service of any such personnel, and we fail to recruit replacements with the required knowledge, experience and qualifications to replace them, then our business may be disrupted and our financial condition and results of operations may be adversely affected.

15 The insurance coverage may be inadequate to protect us from potential loss. Hanbo has not purchased any insurance to cover our business. Further, we do not maintain business interruption or key-man life insurance. The occurrence of any of these events may result in our incurring substantial costs and the diversion of our resources. Our insurance coverage may not be sufficient to prevent us from such loss. There is no certainty that we will be able to successfully claim any of our losses under our current insurance policy on a timely basis. If we incur any loss that is not covered by our insurance policies, or the compensated amount is significantly less than our actual loss, our business and financial condition could be materially and adversely affected.

16 Hanbo usually pays the full amount of all costs due to suppliers and third-party manufacturers and arranges for delivery to our customers before we receive payment from our customers. If any significant amount of payments cannot be collected from our customers in the future, our financial conditions and results of operations could be adversely affected. Hanbo also generally arrange for the delivery of apparel products to our customers first, before we receive any payment from our customers and without any deposit as security. We can offer no assurances that all our customers will continuously maintain a good practice of making timely payments to us according to the relevant contractual arrangements. If any significant amount of payments cannot be collected from our customers in the future, for example, due to cancellation of purchase orders, subsequently, our financial conditions and results of operations could be adversely affected. If we adopt a different practice with our customers, such as requiring them to pay before delivery, our relationship with them may deteriorate and they may cease to place orders with us, which may adversely affect our business and financial performance.

17 Hanbo could be subject and may be required to pay the commercial activity tax applicable in Ohio and as a result, its financial condition and operating results may be adversely affected. As advised by our US legal advisers, applicable law is not clear on whether an Ohio gross receipts tax called the commercial activity tax may be applied to non-US entities (such as our Group) based solely on the fact that they ship goods to Ohio. Further, our US legal advisers have advised that such a law may not be applicable to us, as ownership to the apparel products that we procure for our US customers passes from us to our US customers at the shipping point, which is outside of the US, and so, during shipment and delivery in Ohio, we do not own the apparel products. In addition, we have never been contacted by any tax authority in Ohio regarding any possible liability for the commercial

activity tax, and we have never been subject to any audit or assessment of commercial activity tax. Based on the factors stated above, we have decided not to participate in a voluntary disclosure program established in Ohio enabling entities to disclose their possible liability for the commercial activity tax. Entities participating in the voluntary disclosure program will pay the commercial activity tax for the current year and the past three years subject to actual liability plus interest but no penalties will be imposed. If we are found liable for the commercial activity tax without having participated in the voluntary disclosure program, we may be required to pay the commercial activity tax for all the years in which we shipped goods to Ohio. As advised by our US legal advisers, it is estimated that, assuming our participation in the voluntary disclosure program, the maximum amount of our tax liabilities (including applicable interest) would be in the range of US$89,500 to US$98,500. As further advised by our US legal advisers, it is estimated that, assuming we are found liable for the commercial activity tax and we have not participated in the voluntary disclosure program, the maximum amount of our tax liabilities (including applicable late filing charges and interest) would be in the range of US$103,000 to US$113,500 for the Track Record Period and in the range of US$180,000 to US$192,000 for all the years in which we shipped goods to Ohio. If Hanbo is subject to the commercial activity tax, we may be required to pay the commercial activity tax and as a result, our financial condition and operating results may be adversely affected. Hanbo's Directors believe that the apparel products we procured for our customers are distributed and sold by our customers throughout the US within the confines of our customers' sales channels, and that so far as our company is aware, we are potentially subject to tax on our commercial activities only in Ohio.

18 Hanbo experienced incidents of non-compliance with the Predecessor Companies Ordinance. Hanbo has on various occasions not fully complied with statutory requirements in the Predecessor Companies Ordinance with respect to matters such as timely convening of annual general meeting and adoption of audited financial statements. See "Business – Non-compliance incidents" for further details. If the Registrar of Companies in Hong Kong takes any action against the relevant subsidiaries in our Group, including the assessment of fines or other penalties and/or if our Controlling Shareholders fail to indemnify us in full, our reputation, cash flow and results of operations may be adversely affected.

19 Hanbo may be requested to make up any unpaid social insurance fund and housing provident fund contributions during the Track Record Period. Pursuant to the relevant PRC laws and regulations, employers in the PRC are required to make social insurance contributions and housing provident fund contributions for the benefit of their employees, and entities which fail to make contributions may be ordered to settle the unpaid contribution and subject to penalty within a stipulated time limit. During the Track Record Period, we did not make social insurance contributions and housing

provident fund contributions in full for our employees. Hanbo's Directors have assessed that the unpaid amount of contributions to the social insurance and housing provident fund were approximately HK$2.1 million and HK$1.4 million, respectively, up to 31 December 2013. We have been in compliance with the relevant regulations in relation to social insurance contributions since January 2014 and housing provident fund contributions since July 2013. Provision for the unpaid amount has been made in our financial statements in full, which our Directors considered adequate. There is no assurance that Hanbo will not be subject to fines or penalties in the future, and if that happens, Hanbo's financial position may be adversely affected.

20 Hanbo is involved in one ongoing litigation. This and any other litigations or legal proceedings could expose Hanbo to financial liability, divert its resources away from its business and adversely affect its reputation and financial condition. As of the Latest Practicable Date, Hanbo was involved in one ongoing litigation against us by a fabric supplier. Until such proceedings are concluded, Hanbo will incur legal costs in defending the claim. Regardless of the merits of the claim, any time and money spent defending this claim diverts resources away from its business. If Hanbo is found liable, we may have to pay out damages to satisfy the claim. If our Controlling Shareholders fail or are unable to indemnify us against any liabilities arising from the matter pursuant to the Deed of Indemnity, Hanbo may need to bear the full amount of the claim and other interests and costs as we do not have insurance to cover the costs of litigation. As of the Latest Practicable Date, as the trial is yet to be held, the results and outcome of the litigation are inherently uncertain, thus we are unable to accurately quantify the total amount of our liabilities at this stage if we are found liable. Hanbo is subject to the risk of legal claims and proceedings and regulatory enforcement actions in the ordinary course of our business. Any litigations or legal proceedings could expose us to financial liability, divert our resources away from our business and our reputation and financial condition could be adversely affected.

21 Hanbo may not be able to successfully implement our business objectives, and our expansion plans may not be successful. Hanbo's business objectives are accomplished by implementing various future business plans. The Directors believe that its future success depends on our ability to continually expand our base of third-party manufacturers and broaden our product offerings. However, such expansion plan is formulated based on assumptions as to the occurrence of certain future events, which may or may not materialize, and thus it is subject to a series of uncertainties and risks, including but not limited to: (1) lack of sufficient capital financing and potential ongoing financial obligations; (2) failure to achieve the intended level of profitability; (3) delays or difficulties in securing suitable new third-party manufacturers; and (4) diversion of resources and management attention. As such, there is no assurance that our expansion plan will materialize within

the planned timeframe, or at all, or that our business objectives will be fully or partially accomplished. In the event that we fail to accomplish our expansion plan or to do so in a timely manner, we may not be able to achieve our planned future business growth, and our operating results may be adversely affected. We expect to incur significant costs in connection with the expansion of our business. If we are unable to generate sufficient revenue from our business or our financial needs are larger than expected, we may need to raise funds from debt or equity financing means. Alternatively, we may need to make certain modifications to our current intended use of proceeds, which could have an adverse effect on our operations and future profitability. We also face the risk that our existing management staff, design and development capabilities, and internal control systems and other systems and procedures may be inadequate to support our expansion plan. If we fail to continue to improve our infrastructure, management or operational systems required to support our expansion plan, we may be unable to achieve our expansion objectives and our business operations may be seriously harmed.

22 There is a possible impact of certain non-recurring expenses on Hanbo's financial performance. Notwithstanding our financial performance for the three years between 2011 and 2013 disclosed in this prospectus, our financial results for the year ending 31 December 2014 will be affected by certain non-recurring expenses, including the expenses in relation to the Listing. Currently, we only have an estimate of our listing expenses to be incurred, and the actual amount to be recognized in the financial statements of our Group for the year ending 31 December 2014 is subject to adjustment based on the audit and the changes in variables and assumptions. Accordingly, our financial results for the year ending 31 December 2014 will be affected by the expenses in relation to the Listing.

23 If Hanbo fails to collect its receivables (other than trade and bills receivables), its financial condition and results of operations may be materially and adversely affected. Hanbo recorded receivables (other than trade and bills receivables) during the Track Record Period, which amounted to approximately HK$48.5 million, HK$61.0 million and HK$46.7 million as of 31 December 2011, 2012 and 2013 respectively. (Such receivables are referred to as 'other receivables' in "Financial Information – Net current assets – Prepayments, deposits and other receivables" and are discussed therein). We cannot assure you that we will be able to collect such other receivables from our debtors, including the relevant third-party manufacturers, in full or in a timely manner, and our failure to do so may materially and adversely affect our financial condition, results of operations and cash flow, as we could be forced to write off a receivable in accordance with IFRS and our accounting policies if our debtors failed to honor their repayment obligations. In addition, we may incur expenses and have management resources diverted relating to the collection of such other receivables, such as through legal proceedings.

24 Hanbo may not be able to sustain our historical financial performance and may encounter difficulties in sustaining profitability. The total revenue amounted to approximately HK$666.7 million, HK$463.6 million and HK$554.6 million as of 31 December 2011, 2012 and 2013 respectively. The gross profit for the same period was approximately HK$85.1 million, HK$73.2 million and HK$84.6 million respectively. The gross profit margin for each of the same period was approximately 12.8 percent, 15.8 percent and 15.3 percent respectively. The net profit margin was 3.0 percent, 6.2 percent and 4.5 percent for the same period. However, the revenue and profit during the Track Record Period may not be indicative of our future performance, and we may encounter difficulties in sustaining our current profitability. Our future revenue and profitability depend on a number of factors, including the successful implementation of our future plans as stated in "Future plans and use of proceeds". Our gross and net profit margins also depend on factors, including the selling prices of our products and sales volumes that are outside of our control, and therefore we cannot assure you that we will be able to maintain the current level of profit margins in the future. Investors should be aware that we can offer no assurances that we will be able to increase or maintain our historical revenue or profit levels.

25 Hanbo may not be able to successfully track the fast changing fashion trends and respond to customer demands for garment products. During the Track Record Period, we sourced mainly woven wear products for our customers. We cannot accurately predict the supply and demand for particular garment products that may change from season to season and from year to year due to factors such as fashion trends or fluctuations in consumer preferences. If consumer demand for woven wear products decrease, our customers may reduce the size of orders placed with us or cease to place orders with us, and our operating results may be materially and adversely affected due to fluctuation in purchase orders. If we are unable to predict, identify and respond promptly to such changes, we may not be able to adjust our operations to cope in a timely manner. For example, we may not be able to locate third-party manufacturers to produce other types of garment products that meet our requirements, and we may not have sufficient time to recruit suitable personnel or introduce appropriate changes to our operation model.

26 Hanbo cannot guarantee the accuracy of facts, projections, other statistics and information derived from various official government publications or obtained from Ipsos from the Industry Expert Report, referred to in this book. Facts, projections, other statistics and information in this prospectus relating to the global and US market and the apparel supply chain management services industry have been derived from various official PRC government publications or obtained from Ipsos. We believe that these publications are appropriate sources for such information and have taken reasonable care in extracting and reproducing such information. We have no reason to believe that such information is false or misleading or that any fact has been

omitted that would render such information false or misleading. However, we cannot guarantee the quality or reliability of the source materials. They have not been prepared or independently verified by us, the Sponsor, the Bookrunner and Lead Manager and the Underwriters or any of our or their respective affiliates or advisers and, therefore, we make no representation as to the accuracy of such facts, forecasts, statistics and information, which may not be consistent with other information compiled elsewhere. Due to possibly flawed or ineffective collection methods or discrepancies between published information and market practice, the facts, forecasts, statistics and information in this prospectus may be inaccurate or may not be comparable to facts, forecasts, statistics and information produced with respect to other economies. Furthermore, we cannot assure you that they are stated or compiled on the same basis or with the same degree of accuracy as may be the case elsewhere. Hence, you should not unduly rely upon the facts, forecasts, statistics and information with respect to the global and US market and the apparel supply chain management services industry contained in this book.

8.6.2   *Risks relating to apparel industry*

1   *The sales may be affected by seasonality.* Any seasonal fluctuations may affect the number of orders that customers place with us and may not match our expectations, which could adversely affect our financial conditions and results of operation. Our sales are subject to seasonal fluctuations during the year and are largely determined in part by two major fashion seasons: Spring/Summer and Autumn/Winter. We generally record higher sales from December to April for the Spring/Summer products as our customers have higher demand for our major product of woven wear such as shirts and blouses for their Spring/Summer collections. These fluctuations may vary considerably from time to time as a result of changes in seasonal demand. As a result of these fluctuations, comparisons of sales and revenue between different periods within the same financial year, or between the same periods in different financial years, are not necessarily meaningful and cannot be relied upon as indicators of our past or future performance. Any seasonal fluctuations reported in the future may not match our expectations and this could adversely affect our company's financial conditions and results of operation.

2   *Fluctuations in consumer spending caused by changes in macroeconomic conditions may significantly affect our business operations, financial condition, results of operations and prospects.* Our customers' purchasing decisions and quantity of orders placed with us will be heavily influenced by the likely spending habits of their consumers. Such spending habits may be influenced by macroeconomic conditions in their country of residence. Changes and developments in global political, economic and financial conditions will in turn affect the volume of our business and performance. If demand from

end consumers is low, companies operating in the apparel supply chain management industry may experience significant reductions in orders and greater pricing pressures from customers. Other factors such as the imposition of new trade barriers, sanctions, boycotts and other measures, trade disputes, labour disputes, disruptions to the transportation industry, as well as acts of war or hostilities, could delay or prevent the delivery of apparel products to customers in the US or elsewhere, or even reduce demand for apparel products. If this were to occur, there would be an adverse effect on our business operations, financial condition, results of operations and prospects.

3   *Increased inspection procedures, tighter import and export controls and additional trade restrictions could increase our operating costs and cause disruption to our business.* The apparel industry is subject to various security and customs inspections and related procedures (Inspection Procedures) in countries of origin and destination as well as at transshipment points. Such Inspection Procedures can result in the seizure of apparel products and the levying of customs duties, fines or other penalties against exporters or importers. If Inspection Procedures or other controls are further tightened, we may incur further costs and delays and our business could be harmed.

4   *An increase in the minimum wage of apparel-making factory workers and pressure to improve working conditions may adversely affect our business operations and financial condition.* Pressure on the governments in countries including Bangladesh and Cambodia to increase the minimum wage of workers in apparel-making factories could increase the operating costs of our third-party manufacturers. This increase may then be passed on to Hanbo through an increase in subcontracting fees. If we are not able to pass on such additional costs to our customers, this may adversely affect our business operations and financial condition.

8.6.3   *Risks relating to conducting business in the PRC*

The economic, political and social conditions of the PRC, as well as its government policies, could adversely affect the financial markets in the PRC and our business and results of operations. Our operations and financial results could be adversely affected by changes in political, economic and social conditions or the relevant policies of the PRC government, such as changes in laws and regulations (or the interpretations thereof), measures which might be introduced to control inflation, changes in the rate or method of taxation, the imposition of additional restrictions on currency conversion and the imposition of additional export restrictions. Furthermore, a significant portion of economic activities in the PRC are export-driven at present and, therefore, are affected by developments in the economies of the principal trading partners of the PRC and other export-driven economies. Since late 2003, the PRC government has implemented a number of measures to prevent the PRC economy from overheating. While some of these measures may benefit the overall PRC economy, they may have a negative effect on us. Many of the economic reforms undertaken by the PRC government are unprecedented, and they may be subject to change, revision or abolition. We can offer no assurance that the PRC government will continue to pursue a policy of economic reform. The policies and other measures taken by the PRC government to regulate the PRC economy may adversely affect our operating and financial results.

1　The PRC's legal system is still evolving and the uncertainties as to the interpretation and enforcement of PRC laws could have a material adverse effect on apparel industry. Some of our business and operations are conducted in China, and thus we are governed primarily by PRC laws and regulations. The PRC legal system is a civil law system based on written statutes and past court decisions have limited precedential value and are cited for reference only. Since the late 1970s, the PRC government has made significant progress in the development of its laws and regulations governing economic matters, such as foreign investment, company organization and management, business, tax and trade. As these laws and regulations are still evolving and there are only limited number of non-binding court cases, however, there exist uncertainties about the interpretation and enforcement of the laws and regulations. For the same reasons, any legal protections available to us under these laws and regulations may be limited. Any litigation or regulatory enforcement action in China may be protracted and could result in substantial costs and diversion of resources and management attention.

2　The enforcement of the labour-related regulations in the PRC such as the Labour Contract Law of the PRC may adversely affect our business and our results of operations. Compared to the Labour Law of the PRC, the Labour Contract Law of the PRC (the **Labour Contract Law**), enacted by the National People's Congress of the PRC on 29 June 2007 and implemented on 1 January 2008, has more stringent requirements on employers in relation to entry into fixed-term employment contracts and dismissal of employees. Overall, the Labour Contract Law includes specific provisions related to fixed-term employment contracts, temporary employment, probation, consultation with labour unions and employee general assemblies, employment without a contract, dismissal of employees, compensation upon termination and overtime work, and collective bargaining. Under the Labour Contract Law, an employer is required to sign an unlimited term labour contract with an employee if the employer continues to employ the employee after the expiration of two consecutive fixed-term labour contracts except in certain circumstances as specified in the Labour Contract Law. An employer is also required to make severance payments to fixed-term contract employees when the term of their employment contracts expire, except in certain circumstances as prescribed in the Labour Contract Law including where an employee voluntarily rejects an offer to renew the contract when the conditions offered by the employer are the same as or better than those stipulated in the current contract. In addition, employees have the right to receive overtime wages when working overtime and the right to terminate or modify the terms of the labour contracts under the Labour Contract Law. In addition, under the Regulations on Paid Annual Leave for Employees, which was implemented on 1 January 2008, employees who have served more than one year with an employer are entitled to paid vacation ranging from five to 15 days, depending on their length of service. Employees who agree to waive their holiday time at the request of their employers must be compensated with three times their normal daily salary for each day of holiday waived. As a result of these labour protective measures, our historical labour costs may not be indicative of our labour costs going forward, and there can be no assurance that there will not be any additional or new labour laws, rules or regulations in the PRC, which may lead to potential increases in labour costs or future disputes with our employees. There can also be no assurance that any disputes, work stoppages or strikes will not arise in the future. Compliance with the relevant laws and regulations may substantially affect our operating costs, or those of the third-party manufacturers and suppliers, and thus may have a material adverse effect on our results of operations.

3   PRC regulations in relation to direct capital investments and loans by off-shore holding companies to PRC entities may delay or restrict us from using the proceeds from the Global Offering to make additional contributions or loans to our PRC subsidiary. We may use the proceeds of the Global Offering to finance our business by making loans or additional capital contributions to our subsidiary established in the PRC. As a company incorporated in the Cayman Islands, any such capital contribution or loan that we make to our PRC subsidiary are subject to PRC regulations. For example, any of our loans to our PRC subsidiary cannot exceed the difference between the total amount of investment that our PRC subsidiary is approved to make under the relevant PRC laws and the registered capital of our PRC subsidiary and any such loans must be registered with the local branch of SAFE. In addition, if we make additional capital contributions to finance our PRC subsidiary, the amount of these capital contributions must be approved by and registered with the MOFCOM or its local counterpart. We offer no assurance that we will be able to obtain these approvals on a timely basis, or at all. If we fail to receive such approvals, our ability to use the proceeds of the Global Offering and our ability to make capital investments, or provide loans to our PRC subsidiary, or to fund and expand its operations could be adversely affected, which could have a material adverse effect on our PRC subsidiary's liquidity, its ability to fund its working capital requirements and our overall business, results of operations and financial condition.

4   The apparel industry may rely on dividends and other distributions on equity paid by our PRC subsidiary to fund any cash and financing requirements we may have, and any limitation on the ability of our PRC subsidiary

to make payments to us could have a material adverse effect on our ability to conduct our business. Hanbo is a holding company and may rely on dividends paid by our PRC subsidiary for our cash requirements. Current PRC regulations permit our PRC subsidiary to pay dividends to us only out of its retained earnings, if any, determined in accordance with PRC accounting standards. In addition, our PRC subsidiary is required to set aside a certain percentage of its after-tax profits based on PRC accounting standards each year to its reserve fund until the accumulated amount has reached 50 percent of the registered capital of our PRC subsidiary, in accordance with the requirements of relevant laws and provisions in its articles of association. These reserves, however, are not allowed to be distributed as cash dividends. Furthermore, if our PRC subsidiary incurs debt on its own behalf, the instruments governing the debt could restrict its ability to pay dividends or make other payments to us. As a result, our PRC subsidiary is restricted in its ability to transfer a portion of its net income to us, whether in the form of dividends, loans or advances, which could adversely affect our business operations.

5   The apparel industry faces taxation uncertainty with respect to the indirect transfer of equity interests in our PRC resident enterprise through transfers made by our non-PRC Shareholders. The State Administration of Taxation (SAT) No. 698, the Notice on Strengthening Administration of Enterprise Income Tax for Share Transfers by Non-PRC Resident Enterprises (Circular 698) on 10 December 2009 which was made retrospectively effective from 1 January 2008. Pursuant to Circular 698 and SAT announcement 2011 No. 24, except for the purchase and sale of equity in a PRC resident enterprise through a public securities market, where a non-PRC resident enterprise (the actual controlling party) indirectly transfers the equity interests of a PRC resident enterprise through disposing of its equity interests in a non-PRC holding company (the Indirect Transfer), and such non-PRC holding company is located in a tax jurisdiction that (1) has either an effective tax rate of less than 12.5 percent, or (2) does not tax foreign income on its residents, the non-PRC resident enterprise shall report the Indirect Transfer to the competent tax authority of the PRC resident. In connection with our reorganization, we conducted a transaction that may be deemed to be an Indirect Transfer of equity interests in our PRC subsidiary, Yibao Clothing. If the relevant PRC tax authorities hold that the non-PRC holding company does not have any bona fide commercial purpose and the Indirect Transfer was conducted for the purpose of avoiding PRC tax, or if the Indirect Transfer is otherwise taxable under Circular 698, the transferor (i.e. Happy Zone) may be required to pay PRC withholding tax for the Indirect Transfer and we may be required to assist Happy Zone in respect of its obligations to file the required documents with, and to pay PRC withholding tax to, the relevant PRC tax authorities. Since the implementation of Circular 698 may, in practice, vary across different local tax authorities, it remains uncertain how the PRC tax authorities will examine the commercial purpose of

non-PRC holding companies and Indirect Transfers generally. The extent to which we may be required to assist Happy Zone in its filing and payment obligations is not stipulated in any definitive PRC law and is subject to the discretion of the relevant PRC tax authority. If we are required by the relevant PRC tax authority to assist Happy Zone in respect of its obligations to pay withholding tax, our tax liability may increase and our business operations, financial condition and operating results may be adversely affected. Notwithstanding, according to Circular 698, the reporting and tax obligation, if any, remains with the transferor, i.e. Happy Zone in our case.

6   The apparel industry may experience difficulty in effecting service of legal process, enforcing any judgments or bringing original actions in the PRC or Hong Kong based on foreign laws against us and our Directors and senior management. Hanbo is incorporated in the Cayman Islands. A portion of our assets are located in the PRC and are subject to the PRC legal framework that is materially different from other jurisdictions, including Hong Kong and the US. Therefore, it may not be possible for investors to effect service of process upon us inside the PRC. The PRC has not entered into treaties or arrangements providing for the recognition and enforcement of judgments made by courts of most other jurisdictions. On 14 July 2006, Hong Kong and the PRC entered into the Arrangement on Reciprocal Recognition and Enforcement of Judgments in Civil and Commercial Matters by the Courts of the Mainland and of the Hong Kong Special Administrative Region Pursuant to Choice of Court Agreements Between Parties Concerned (the Arrangement), pursuant to which a party with a final court judgment rendered by a Hong Kong court requiring payment of money in a civil and commercial case according to a choice of court agreement in writing may apply for recognition and enforcement of the judgment in the PRC. Similarly, a party with a final judgment rendered by a PRC court requiring payment of money in a civil and commercial case pursuant to a choice of court agreement in writing may apply for recognition and enforcement of such judgment in Hong Kong. A choice of court agreement in writing is defined as any agreement in writing entered into between parties after the effective date of the Arrangement in which a Hong Kong court or a PRC court is expressly designated as the court having sole jurisdiction for the dispute. Therefore, it may not be possible to enforce a judgment rendered by a Hong Kong court in the PRC if the parties in the dispute do not agree to enter into a choice of court agreement in writing. As a result, it may be difficult or impossible for investors to effect service of process against our assets in the PRC in order to seek recognition and enforcement of foreign judgments in the PRC.

7   Dividends payable by the apparel industry to the foreign investors and gain on the sale of our Shares by our foreign investors may become subject to withholding income tax under PRC tax laws. Under the EIT Law and the implementation rules issued by the State Council, PRC withholding income tax at the rate of 10.0 percent is applicable to dividends payable by a PRC tax resident enterprise to investors that are 'non-PRC resident enterprises'.

Under these laws, if we are deemed to be a non-PRC tax resident enterprise that does not have an establishment or place of business in the PRC, or we do have such establishment or place of business, but the relevant income is not effectively connected with the establishment or place of business, then withholding income tax at the rate of 10.0 percent will be applicable to any dividends paid from our PRC subsidiary to us unless we are entitled to a reduction or elimination of such tax under applicable tax treaties. Similarly, any gain realized on the transfer of shares of a PRC tax resident enterprise by such investors is also subject to 10.0 percent PRC withholding income tax if such gain is regarded as income derived from sources within the PRC. Investors who are established in Hong Kong and are considered as non-PRC resident enterprises by the PRC tax authority are subject to a PRC withholding income tax at a reduced rate of 5.0 percent if the investor is qualified as the beneficial owner and owns more than 25.0 percent of the registered capital of the PRC tax resident enterprise. If we are deemed a PRC 'resident enterprise' under the EIT Law, it is unclear whether the dividends we pay with respect to the Shares, or the gain our foreign Shareholders (excluding individual natural persons) may realize from the sale of Shares may be treated as income derived from sources within the PRC and be subject to PRC income tax. If we are required under the EIT Law to withhold PRC income tax on our dividends payable to our foreign Shareholders, or if they are required to pay PRC income tax on the transfer of the Shares, the value of their investment in our Shares may be adversely affected.

8   The apparel industry faces risks related to health epidemics and other outbreaks of contagious diseases, including avian flu, SARS and swine flu. Our business could be adversely affected by the effects of avian flu, SARS, swine flu or another epidemic or outbreak of communicable diseases. During April 2013, there were outbreaks of highly pathogenic avian flu, caused by the H7N9 virus in certain parts of the PRC. In early 2009, there were reports of outbreaks of a highly pathogenic swine flu, caused by the H1N1 virus in certain regions of Asia and Europe. An outbreak of contagious diseases in the PRC or elsewhere could have a material adverse effect on our business operations, or those of our third-party manufacturers and suppliers. This could include restrictions on travel or the shipment of apparel products outside of the PRC or prevent our staff from travelling to customers' offices to discuss product designs or product samples. If any epidemic or outbreak of communicable diseases were to occur in the future, our business operations could be adversely affected.

8.6.4   *Risks relating to conducting business in countries other than the PRC*

The non-PRC operations subject Hanbo to additional local laws and regulations, government policies and economic, social and political conditions of the respective jurisdictions in which we operate. Apart from our operations in the PRC, we have operations in Hong Kong, Macao, Cambodia and Bangladesh. We may be subject to the local laws and regulations in the respective jurisdictions in which we operate. Any change to the relevant local government regulations or policies, whether relating to labour safety, tax treatment, environmental protection or any other aspects, may directly affect the operating costs of our sales. In addition, any political unrest could directly or indirectly cause strikes or labour unrest and could substantially disrupt our business and operations. This may in turn adversely affect our profitability and financial results.

1   *Risks relating to our business operations involving US customers.* We rely significantly on the US market and any changes in the economic and regulatory conditions of the US, or changes in the business strategy of our US customers, may have a material impact on our business. Almost all of our customers, including our five largest customers for the Track Record Period, are retailers or specialty stores in the US who sell apparel products either directly to the US domestic market or in other countries. Revenue generated from the US market accounted for approximately 91.0 percent, 90.4 percent and 88.6 percent of our total revenue from 2011 to 2013, while revenue from the sales to other markets accounted for approximately 9.0 percent, 9.6 percent and 11.4 percent of our total revenue for the same periods respectively. If there is any change in the economic conditions of the US or any change in the management or control of our US customers, then our US customers may change their business strategies, which may cause their demand for apparel products that we procure for them to decrease, and this may have an adverse effect on our business performance, financial condition and results of operations. We do not have direct contractual arrangements with the end-users who are the consumers of our customers. Our sales to our customers are made on an order-by-order basis. For example, there may be a serious downturn in the overall economy of the US or in the US apparel retail industry; measures to tighten the US credit policy may be introduced to control inflation in the US; and policies unfavorable to the import of goods into the US may deteriorate the financial condition and purchasing power of our customers in the US. In addition, during periods of economic or political uncertainty (such as the conflicts in Afghanistan, Iraq and Syria), orders placed by our US customers may be reduced. Our customers are not obliged to place orders with us, so order quantities can fluctuate depending on the profitability of our customers' businesses and their spending power. A renewed economic downturn in the US or continued uncertainties regarding future prospects that affect consumer spending habits in the US may have an adverse effect on the placing of orders by our customers. We can offer no assurances that we will be able to respond quickly to any economic, market or regulatory changes in the US market, and any failure to do so may cause an adverse effect on our business performance, financial condition and results of operations.

2   *Risks relating to conducting business in Macao.* Conducting business in Macao involves certain risks not typically associated with operations in Hong Kong, including risks relating to changes in Macao's and the PRC's political, economic and social conditions, changes in Macao governmental policies, changes in Macao laws or regulations or their interpretation, changes in interest rate and change in rates or method of taxation. Our operations in Macao are exposed to the risk of changes in laws and policies that govern companies that operate in Macao. In addition, the legal and judicial system adopted in Macao is substantially different from that in Hong Kong, and rights and protections under Hong Kong laws that companies in Hong Kong expect, may not exist in Macao.

3   *Risk relating to conducting business in Cambodia.* Our business may be subject to labour unrest and political unrest in Cambodia that may adversely affect our business and operations. Our operations in Cambodia are subject to laws, rules and regulations promulgated by the Cambodian Parliament or the Cambodian Government. The laws in Cambodia and its legal system are still in a developmental stage and are subject to change. This means there is a lack of consistency and predictability in dispute resolution and in the interpretation and enforcement of laws and regulations. Accordingly, conducting business in Cambodia entails a certain degree of risk and uncertainty. In the event that new laws are imposed, or existing laws, rules or regulations are interpreted or enforced in a way that is adverse to our operations, our business could be adversely affected. Furthermore, the recent history of Cambodia has been characterized by political instability, with ongoing protests between different factions over claims of widespread electoral rigging since the general election that took place in July 2013. Additionally, during the Track Record Period, there were increased demands from garment factory workers for better pay and working conditions. Hence, labour market risks are high in Cambodia, mainly reflecting the increased incidence of labour unrest and the limited supply of skilled labour in Cambodia. The incidence of labour unrest may increase costs for the third-party manufacturers in Cambodia, which they may pass on to us, or, on the part of the third-party manufacturers, may result in the disruption to production schedules or closure of production sites, which may adversely affect our ability to deliver apparel products to our customers on time. Further increases in the minimum wage of Cambodian textile and garment sector workers and pressure to improve working conditions may also adversely affect our business operations and financial condition. Further, infrastructure in Cambodia is poorly developed, and this presents a high risk to businesses operating in Cambodia. There are also moderate security risks stemming from violent and organized crime, increasing social unrest related to the recent election in July 2013 and demands for increases in the minimum wage. Any of these risks could adversely affect our business operations or those of the third-party manufacturers in Cambodia.

4   *Risk relating to conducting business in Bangladesh.* Our business may be subject to labour unrest and political unrest in Bangladesh that may adversely affect our business and operations. Bangladesh is susceptible to power shortages. Our information technology and administrative systems need electricity to function, and power outages could not only disrupt our operations and result in loss of revenue, but they could also cause inefficiency and an increase of waste. The textiles and apparels sector of Bangladesh is heavily affected by labour unrest. Any incident of labour unrest may increase costs for the third-party manufacturers in Bangladesh, which they may pass on to us, or adversely affect our ability to deliver apparel products to our customers on time. In addition, outbreaks of political unrest (such as the violence and disruption related to the national elections in Bangladesh in January 2014) may result in labour strikes and closures of the production facilities of the third-party manufacturers in Bangladesh which may disrupt production schedules or adversely affect our ability to deliver apparel products to our customers on time. As a result, power outages, labour unrest or political unrest in Bangladesh could adversely affect our business and operations.

8.7   Factors affecting Hanbo's financial conditions and results of operation

1   Change in economic conditions in the US
2   Reliance on our major customers during the Track Record Period
3   Cost fluctuations
4   Use of third-party manufacturers
5   Lack of long-term agreements with our customers
6   Payment arrangements
7   Seasonality of our apparel products
8   Changes in government policies and regulations in Macao and in other jurisdictions
9   Commercial activity tax applicable in Ohio

References

Aghezzaf, E. (2005). Capacity planning and warehouse location in supply chains with uncertain demands. *The Journal of the Operational Research Society*, 56(4), 453–462.

Ambulkar, S., Blackhurst, J.V. and Cantor, D.E. (2016). Supply chain risk mitigation competency: An individual-level knowledge-based perspective. *International Journal of Production Research*, 54(5), 1398–1411.

Amid, A., Ghodsypour, S.H. and O'Brien, C. (2006). Fuzzy multiobjective linear model for supplier selection in a supply chain. *International Journal of Production Economics*, 104(2), 394–407.

Amid, A., Ghodsypour, S.H. and O'Brien, C. (2011). A weighted max-min model for fuzzy multi-objective supplier selection in a supply chain. *International Journal of Production Economics*, 131(1), 139–145.

Amin, S.H., Razmi, J. and Zhang, G. (2011). Supplier selection and order allocation based on fuzzy SWOT analysis and fuzzy linear programming. *Expert Systems with Applications*, 38(1), 334–342.

Aqlan, F. and Lam, S.S. (2015). Supply chain risk modelling and mitigation. *International Journal of Production Research*, 53(18), 5640–5656.

Audet, D. (2004). *A New World Map in Textiles and Clothing Policy Brief*, Organization for Economic Co-operation and Development (OECD), Washington, DC.

Azadnia, A.H., Sam, M.Z.M. and Wong, K.Y. (2015). Sustainable supplier selection and order lot-sizing: An integrated multi-objective decision-making process. *International Journal of Production Research*, 53(2), 383–408.

Barron, F.H. and Barrett, B.E. (1996). Decision quality using ranked attribute weights. *Management Science*, 42(11), 1515–1523.

Bayrak, M.Y., Celebi, N. and Taskin, H. (2007). A fuzzy approach method for supplier selection. *Production Planning & Control*, 18(1), 54–63.

Beil, D.R. (2010). Supplier selection. *Wiley Encyclopedia of Operation Research and Management Science*. doi: 10.1002/9780470400531.eorms0852, 1–21.

Benjaafar, A., Elahi, E. and Donohue, K.L. (2007). Outsourcing via service competition. *Management Sciences*, 53(2), 241–259.

Ben-Tal, A. and Nemirovski, A. (1998). Robust convex optimization. *Mathematics of Operations Research*, 23(4), 769–805.

Ben-Tal, A. and Nemirovski, A. (1999). Robust solutions of uncertain linear programs. *Operations Research Letters*, 25(1), 1–13.

Ben-Tal, A. and Nemirovski, A. (2000). Robust solutions of linear programming problems contaminated with uncertain data. *Mathematical Programming*, 88(3), 411–424.

Ben-Tal, A. and Nemirovski, A. (2002). Robust optimization – methodology and applications. *Mathematical Programming*, 92(3), 453–480.

Bertsimas, D. and Sim, M. (2003). Robust discrete optimization and network flows. *Mathematical Programming*, 98(1–3), 49–71.

Bertsimas, D. and Sim, M. (2004). The price of robustness. *Operations Research*, 52(1), 35–53.

Beynon, M.J. (2005). A method of aggregation in DS/AHP for group decision-making with the non-equivalent importance of individuals in the group. *Computers & Operations Research*, 32(7), 1881–1896.

Blome, C. and Schoenherr, T. (2011). Supply chain risk management in financial crisis: A multiple case-study approach. *International Journal of Production Economics*, 134(1), 43–57.

Cao, Q. and Wang, Q. (2007). Optimizing vendor selection in a two-stage outsourcing process. *Computers & Operations Research*, 34(12), 3757–3768.

Cao, X., Fu, Y., Du, J., Sun, J. and Wang, M. (2016). Measuring Olympics performance based on a distance-based approach. *International Transactions in Operational Research*, 23(5), 979–990.

Chai, J., Liu, J.N.K. and Ngai, E.W.T. (2013). Application of decision-making techniques in supplier selection: A systematic review of literature. *Expert Systems with Applications*, 40(10), 3872–3885.

Chand, M., Raj, T. and Shanker, R. (2015). A comparative study of multi criteria decision making approaches for risks assessment in supply chain. *International Journal of Business Information Systems*, 18(1), 67–84.

Chen, C.T., Lin, C.T. and Huang, S.F. (2006). A fuzzy approach for supplier evaluation and selection in supply chain management. *International Journal of Production Economics*, 102(2), 289–301.

Chen, P.-S. and Wu, M.-T. (2013). A modified failure mode and effects analysis method for supplier selection problems in the supply chain risk environment: A case study. *Computers & Industrial Engineering*, 66(4), 634–642.

Christopher, M. and Lee, H. (2004). Mitigating supply chain risk through improved confidence. *International Journal of Physical Distribution & Logistics Management*, 34(5), 388–396.

Chu, A.W.T., Kalaba, R.E. and Spingarn, K. (1979). A comparison of two methods for determining the weights of belonging to fuzzy sets. *Journal of Optimization Theory and Applications*, 27(4), 531–538.

Colicchia, C. and Strozzi, F. (2012). Supply chain risk management: A new methodology for a systematic literature review. *Supply Chain Management: An International Journal*, 17(4), 403–418.

Cucchiella, F. and Gastaldi, M. (2006). Risk management in supply chain: A real option approach. *Journal of Manufacturing Technology Management*, 17(6), 700–720.

Demitras, E.A. and Üstün, Ö. (2008). An integrated multiobjective decision making process for supplier selection and order allocation. *Omega*, 36(1), 76–90.

Denton, B.T., Miller, A.J., Balasubramanian, H.J. and Huschka, T.R. (2010). Optimal allocation of surgery blocks to operating rooms under uncertainty. *Operations Research*, 58(4, part 1), 802–816.

Diabat, A., Govindan, W. and Panicker, V.V. (2012). Supply chain risk management and its mitigation in a food industry. *International Journal of Production Research*, 50(11), 3039–3050.

Diakoulaki, D., Mavrotas, G. and Papayannaskis, L. (1995). Determining objective weights in multiple criteria problems: The critic method. *Computers & Operations Research*, 22(7), 763–770.

Dickson, G.W. (1966). An analysis of vendor selection systems and decisions. *Journal of Purchasing*, 2, 5–17.

Düzgün, R. and Thile, A. (2010). Robust Optimization with Multiple Ranges: Theory and Application to R&D Project Selection, Technical Report, Lehigh University, Bethlehem, PA, USA.

Escudero, L.F., Kamesam, P.V., King, A. and Wets, R.J. (1993). Production planning via scenario modeling. *Annals of Operations Research*, 43(6), 311–335.

Finch, P. (2004). Supply chain risk management. *Supply Chain Management: An International Journal*, 9(2), 183–196.

Fu, Y., Lai, K.K., Leung, J.W.K. and Liang, L. (2016). A distance-based decision making method to improve multiple criteria supplier selection. *Proceedings of the Institution of Mechanical Engineers, Part B: Journal of Engineering Manufacture*, 230(7), 1351–1355.

Fu, Y., Lai, K.K., Miao, Y. and Leung, J.W.K. (2016). A distance-based decision making method to improve multiple criteria ABC inventory classification. *International Transactions in Operational Research*, 23(5), 969–978.

Fu, Y., Sun, J., Lai, K.K. and Leung, J.W.K. (2015). A robust optimization solution to bottleneck generalized assignment problem under uncertainty. *Annals of Operations Research*, 233(1), 123–133.

Gabrel, V., Murat, C. and Thiele, A. (2014). Recent advances in robust optimization: an overview. *European Journal of Operational Research*, 235(3), 471–483.

Ge, H., Nolan, J., Gray, R., Goetz, S. and Han, Y. (2016). Supply chain complexity and risk mitigation: A hybrid optimization–simulation model. *International Journal of Production Economics*, 179, 228–238.

Gereffi, G. (1999). International trade and industrial upgrading in the apparel commodity chain. *Journal of International Economics*, 48(1), 37–70.

Gereffi, G. and Frederick, S. (2010). The Global Apparel Value Chain, Trade and the Crisis- Challenges and Opportunities for Developing Countries, Policy Research Working Paper, The World Bank Development Research Group Trade and Integration Team, April 2010.

Ghadge, A., Dani, S., Ojha, R. and Caldwell, N. (2017). Using risk sharing contracts for supply chain risk mitigation: A buyer-supplier power and dependence perspective. *Computers & Industrial Engineering*, 103, 262–270.

Ghodsypour, S.H. and O'Brien, C. (2001). The total cost of logistics in supplier selection, under conditions of multiple sourcing, multiple criteria and capacity constraint. *International Journal of Production Economics*, 73(1), 15–27.

Haq, A.N. and Kannan, G. (2006). Fuzzy analytical hierarchy process for evaluating and selecting a vendor in a supply chain model. *The International Journal of Advanced Manufacturing Technology*, 29(7), 826–835.

Heckmann, I., Comes, T. and Nickel, S. (2015). A critical review on supply chain risk: Definition, measure and modeling. *Omega*, 52, 119–132.

Ho, W., Xu, X.W. and Dey, P.K. (2010). Multi-criteria decision making approaches for supplier evaluation and selection: A literature review. *European Journal of Operational Research*, 202(1), 16–24.

Ho, W., Zheng, T., Yildiz, H. and Talluri, S. (2015). Supply chain risk management: A literature review. *International Journal of Production Research*, 53(16), 5031–5069.

Hwang, C.L. and Yoon, K. (1981). *Multiple Attribute Decision-Making: Methods and Applications*, Springer, Berlin.

Jain, N., Girotra, K. and Netessine, S. (2014). Managing global sourcing: Inventory performance. *Management Science*, 60(5), 1202–1222.

José Alem, D. and Morabito, R. (2012). Production planning in furniture settings via robust optimization. *Computers & Operations Research*, 39(2), 139–150.

Jüttner, U., Peck, H. and Christopher, M. (2003). Supply chain risk management: Outlining an agenda for future research. *International Journal of Logistics: Research and Applications*, 6(4), 197–210.

Kasilingam, R.G. and Lee, C.P. (1996). Selection of vendors: A mixed-integer programming approach. *Computers & Industrial Engineering*, 31(1–2), 347–350.

Khan, O. and Yurt, O. (2011). Approaches to managing global sourcing risk. *Supply Chain Management: An International Journal*, 16(2), 67–81.

Kleindorfer, P.R. and Saad, G.H. (2005). Managing disruption risks in supply chains. *Production and Operations Management*, 14(1), 53–68.

Konno, H. and Yamazaki, H. (1999). Mean-absolute deviation portfolio optimization model and its applications to Tokyo stock market. *Management Science*, 37(5), 519–531.

Kumar, M., Vrat, P. and Shankar, R. (2004). A fuzzy goal programming approach for vendor selection problem in a supply chain. *Computers & Industrial Engineering*, 46(1), 69–85.

Kumar, M., Vrat, P. and Shankar, R. (2006). A fuzzy goal programming approach for vendor selection problem in a supply chain. *International Journal of Production Economics*, 101(2), 273–285.

Kuo, R.J., Lee, L.Y. and Hu, T.-L. (2010). Developing a supplier selection system through integrating fuzzy AHP and fuzzy DEA: A case study on an auto lighting system company in Taiwan. *Production Planning & Control*, 21(5), 468–484.

Lahdelma, R., Hokkanen, J. and Salminen, P. (1998). SMAA-stochastic multiobjective acceptability analysis. *European Journal of Operational Research*, 106(1), 137–143.

Lahdelma, R. and Salminen, P. (2001). SMAA-2: Stochastic multicriteria acceptability analysis for group decision making. *Operation Research*, 49(3), 444–454.

Lai, K.K., and Ng. W.L. (2005). A stochastic approach to hotel revenue optimization. *European Journal of Operational Research*, 32(5), 1059–1072.

Lai, K.K., Wang, M. and Liang, L. (2007). A stochastic approach to professional services firms' revenue optimization. *European Journal of Operational Research*, 182(3), 971–982.

Leung, S.C.H., Wu, Y. and Lai, K.K. (2002). A robust optimization model for a cross-border logistics problem with fleet composition in an uncertain environment. *Mathematical and Computer Modelling*, 36(11-13), 1221–1234.

Leung, S.C.H. and Wu, Y. (2004). A robust optimization model for stochastic aggregate production planning. *Production Planning & Control*, 15(5), 502–514.

Liang, L., Wu, J., Cook, W.D. and Zhu, J. (2008). Alternative secondary goals in DEA cross-efficiency evaluation. *International Journal of Production Economics*, 113(2), 1025–1030.

Lim, A., Qin, H. and Xu, Z. (2011). The freight allocation problem lane cost balancing constraint. *European Journal of Operational Research*, 217(1), 26–35.

Lin, X., Janak, S.L. and Floudas, C.A. (2004). A new robust optimization approach for scheduling under uncertainty: I. bounded uncertainty. *Computers & Chemical Engineering*, 28(6–7), 1069–1085.

Lin, Y.-T., Lin, C.-L., Yu, H.-C. and Tzeng, G.-H. (2010). A novel hybrid MCDM approach for outsourcing vendor selection: A case study for a semiconductor company in Taiwan. *Expert Systems with Applications*, 37(7), 4796–4804.

Ma, J., Fan, Z.-P. and Huang, L.-H. (1999). A subjective and objective integrated approach to determine attribute weights. *European Journal of Operational Research*, 112(2), 397–404.

Mandal, A. and Deshmukh, S.G. (1994). Vendor selection using interpretive structural modelling (ISM). *International Journal of Operations & Production Management*, 14(6), 52–59.

Manuj, I. and Mentzer, J.T. (2008). Global supply chain risk management strategies. *International Journal of Physical Distribution & Logistics Management*, 38(3), 192–223.

Michalski, L. (2000). How to identify vendor risk. *Pharmaceutical Technology*, 24(10), 180–184.

Micheli, G.J.L., Mogre, R. and Perego, A. (2014). How to choose mitigation measures for supply chain risks. *International Journal of Production Research*, 52(1), 117–129.

Mula, J., Poler, R., Sabater, G. and Lario, F.C. (2006). Models for production planning under uncertainty: A review. *International Journal of Production Economics*, 103(1), 271–285.

Mulvey, J.M., Vanderbei, R.J. and Zenios, S.A. (1995). Robust optimization of large scale systems. *Operations Research*, 43(2), 264–281.

Nakandala, D., Lau, H. and Zhao, L. (2017). Development of a hybrid fresh food supply chain risk assessment model. *International Journal of Production Research*, 14(55), 4180–4195.

Neiger, D., Rotaru, K. and Churilov, L. (2009). Supply chain risk identification with value-focused process engineering. *Journal of Operations Management*, 27(2), 154–168.

Ng, W.L. (2008). An efficient and simple model for multiple criteria supplier selection problem. *European Journal of Operational Research*, 186(3), 1059–1067.

Olson, D.L. and Wu, D. (2011). Risk management models for supply chain: A scenario analysis of outsourcing to China. *Supply Chain Management: An International Journal*, 16(6), 401–408.

Ordoobadi, S.M. (2009). Development of a supplier selection model using fuzzy logic. *Journal of Supply Chain Management*, 14(4), 314–327.

Paraskevopoulos, D., Karakitsos, E. and Rustem, B. (1991). Robust capacity planning under uncertainty. *Management Science*, 37(7), 787–800.

Peng, C., Wu, X., Fu, Y. and Lai, K.K. (2017). Alternative approaches to constructing composite indicators: An application to construct a sustainable energy index for APEC economies. *Operational Research: An International Journal*, 17(3), 747–759.

Petroin, A. and Braglia, M. (2000). Vendor selection using principal component analysis. *Journal of Supply Chain Management*, 36(1), 63–69.

Pomerol, J.C. and Romero, S.B. (2000). *Multicriteria Decision in Management: Principle and Practice*, Kluwer Academic Publishers.

Pradhan, S.K. and Routroy, S. (2014). Development of supply chain risk mitigation strategy: A case study. *International Journal of Procumbent Management*, 7(4), 359–375.

Rangel, D.A., de Oliveria, T.K. and Leite, M.S.A. (2015). Supply chain risk classification: Discussion and proposal. *International Journal of Production Research*, 53(22), 6868–6887.

Ravindran, A.R., Bilsel, R.U., Wadhaw, V. and Yang, T. (2010). Risk adjusted multicriteria supplier selection models with applications. *International Journal of Production Research*, 48(2), 405–434.

Routroy, S. and Shankar, A. (2014). A study of apparel supply chain risks. *IUP Journal of Supply Chain Management*, 11(2), 52.

Saaty, T.L. (1977). A scaling method for priorities in hierarchical structures. *Journal of Mathematical Psychology*, 15(3), 234–281.

Saaty, T.L. (1980). *The Analytic Hierarchy Process*, McGraw-Hill, New York.

Sadrian, A.A. and Yoon, Y.S. (1994). A procurement decision support system in business volume discount environments. *Operations Research*, 42(1), 14–23.

Sevkli, M. (2010). An application of the fuzzy ELECTRE method for supplier selection. *International Journal of Production Research*, 48(12), 3393–3405.

Shannon, C.E. (1948). A mathematical theory of communication. *Bell System Technical Journal*, 27, 379–423, 623–656.

Shrage, L.E. (1997). Optimization modelling with LINDO. Duxbury Press, Pacific Grove, CA.

Soleimani-damaneh, M. and Zarepisheh, M. (2009). Shannon's entropy for combining the efficiency results of different DEA models: Method and application. *Expert Systems with Applications*, 36(3, part 1), 5146–5150.

Song, W., Ming, X. and Liu, H.-C. (2016). Identifying critical risk factors of sustainable supply chain management: A rough strength-relation analysis method. *Journal of Cleaner Production*, 143, 100–115.

Soyster, A.L. (1973). Convex programming with set-inclusive constraints and applications to inexact linear programming. *Operations Research*, 21(5), 1154–1157.

Steele, P. and Court, B. (1996). *Profitable Purchasing Strategies: A Manger's Guide for Improving Organizational Competitiveness through the Skills of Purchasing*. McGraw-Hill, London.

Sucky, E. (2007). A model for dynamic strategic vendor selection. *Computers & Operations Research*, 34(12), 3638–3651.

Swaminathan, J.M. (2000). Tool capacity planning for semiconductor fabrication facilities under demand uncertainty. *European Journal of Operational Research*, 120(3), 545–558.

Talluri, S. and Narasimhan, R. (2003). Vendor evaluation with performance variability: A max-min approach. *European Journal of Operational Research*, 146(3), 543–552.

Tam, M.C.Y. and Tummala, V.M.R. (2001). An application of the AHP in vendor selection of a telecommunications system. *Omega*, 29(2), 171–182.

Tang, C.S. (2006). Perspective in supply chain risk management. *International Journal of Production Economics*, 103(2), 451–488.

Tang, O. and Musa, S.N. (2011). Identifying risk issues and research advancements in supply chain risk management. *International Journal of Production Economics*, 133(1), 25–34.

Tazelaar, F. and Snijders, C. (2013). Operational risk assessments by supply chain professionals: Process and performance. *Journal of Operations Management*, 31(1–2), 37–51.

Teng, S.G. and Jaramillo, H. (2005). A model for evaluation and selection of suppliers in global textile and apparel supply chains. *International Journal of Physical Distribution & Logistics Management*, 35(7), 503–523.

Tervonen, T. (2014). JSMAA: Open source software for SMAA computations. *International Journal of Systems Science*, 45(1), 69–81.

Tervonen, T. and Lahdelma, R. (2007). Implementing stochastic multicriteria acceptability analysis. *European Journal of Operational Research*, 178(2), 500–513.

Thiele, A. (2004). A Robust Optimization approach to Supply Chain Management and Revenue Management, PhD thesis, MIT, Cambridge, MA.

Tummala, R. and Schoenherr, T. (2011). Assessing and managing risks using the Supply Chain Risk Management Process (SCRMP). *Supply Chain Management: An International Journal*, 16(6), 474–483.

Vilko, J.P.P. and Hallikas, J.M. (2012). Risk assessment in multimodal supply chains. *International Journal of Production Economics*, 140(2), 586–595.

Viswanadham, N. and Samvedi, A. (2013). Supplier selection based on supply chain ecosystem, performance and risk criteria. *International Journal of Production Research*, 51(21), 6484–6498.

Wang, Y.-M. and Luo, Y. (2010). Integration of correlations with standard deviations for determining attribute weights in multiple attribute decision making. *Mathematical and Computer Modelling*, 51(1–2), 1–12.

Wang, Y.-M. and Wang, S. (2013). Approaches to determining the relative importance weights for cross-efficiency aggregation in Data Envelopment Analysis. *Journal of the Operational Research Society*, 64(1), 60–69.

Weber, C.A. and Current, J.R. (1993). A multiobjective approach to vendor selection. *European Journal of Operational Research*, 68(2), 173–184.

Weber, C.A., Current, J.R. and Benton, W.C. (1991). Vendor selection criteria and method. *European Journal of Operational Research*, 50(1), 2–18.

Weber, C.A., Current, J.R. and Desai, A. (1998). Non-cooperative negotiation strategies for vendor selection. *European Journal of Operational Research*, 108(1), 208–223.

Wieland, A. and Wallenburg, C.M. (2012). Dealing with supply chain risks: Linking risk management practices and strategies to performance. *International Journal of Physical Distribution & Logistics Management*, 42(10), 887–905.

Wu, D. and Olson, D.L. (2008). Supply chain risk, simulation, and vendor selection. *International Journal of Production Economics*, 114(2), 646–655.

Wu, D. and Olson, D.L. (2010). Enterprise risk management: A DEA VaR approach in vendor selection. *International Journal of Production Research*, 48(16), 4919–4932.

Wu, J., Sun, J. and Liang, L. (2012). DEA cross-efficiency aggregation method based upon Shannon entropy. *International Journal of Production Research*, 50(23), 6726–6736.

Wu, K.-J., Liao, C.-J., Tseng, M.-L., Lim, M.K., Hu, J. and Tan, K. (2017). Toward sustainability: Using big data to explore the decisive attributes of supply chain risks and uncertainties. *Journal of Cleaner Production*, 142(part 2), 663–676.

Wu, Y. (2011). A stochastic model for production loading in a global apparel manufacturing company under uncertainty. *Production Planning & Control*, 22(3), 269–281.

Yang, F., Ang, S., Xia, Q. and Yang, C.C. (2012). Ranking DMU by interval DEA cross efficiency matrix with acceptability analysis. *European Journal of Operational Research*, 223(2), 483–488.

Yang, J.L., Chiu, H.N., Tzeng, G.-H. and Yeh, R.H. (2008). Vendor selection by integrated fuzzy MCDM techniques with independent and interdependent relationships. *Information Sciences*, 178(21), 4166–4183.

Yu, L. and Lai, K.K. (2011). A distance-based group decision-making methodology for multi-person multi-criteria emergency decision support. *Decision Support Systems*, 51(2), 307–315.

Yu, C.S. and Li, H.L. (2000). A robust optimization model for stochastic logistic problems. *International Journal of Production Economics*, 64(1–3), 385–397.

Zeleny, M. (1982). *Multiple Criteria Decision Making*, McGraw-Hill, New York.

Zsidisin, G.A., Ellram, L.M., Carter, J.R. and Cavinato, J.L. (2004). An analysis of supply risk assessment techniques. *International Journal of Physical Distribution & Logistics Management*, 34(5), 397–413.

Index

Note: Page numbers in italic indicate a figure and page numbers in bold indicate a table on the corresponding page.